SHORT CUTS

INTRODUCTIONS TO FILM STUDIES

1

MISE-EN-SCÈNE

FILM STYLE AND INTERPRETATION

JOHN GIBBS

WALLFLOWER

LONDON and NEW YORK

A Wallflower Paperback

First published in Great Britain in 2002 by Wallflower Press
5 Pond Street, Hampstead, London NW3 2PN
www.wallflowerpress.co.uk

A catalogue record for this book is available from the British Library

ISBN 1 903364 06 X

Book Design by Rob Bowden Design

Printed in Great Britain by Antony Rowe Ltd, Chippenham, Wiltshire

CONTENTS

LIST OF ILLUSTRATIONS

ACKNOWLEDGEMENTS

I would like to thank those who taught me at the Department of Film and Drama at the University of Reading: Jim Hillier, Mike Stevenson, Lib Taylor and Stephen Lacey, Douglas Pye and the late Andrew Britton. I should particularly like to thank Douglas Pye who was a wonderful supervisor; I have benefited enormously from the intelligence and generosity of his teaching, as has this book. Although quite distinct from my thesis, the present book draws on much of the research that went into that project, and on many of the ideas that were shared with me whilst I was working on it. In this regard I am also indebted to Ian Cameron, V.F. Perkins, Charles Barr and Alan Lovell, who consented to be interviewed for the thesis and who provided many valuable observations. I should also like to thank my students and my colleagues at the Film and Television Division at the London College of Printing, who have provided an immensely stimulating environment in which to teach: some very exciting work, practical and critical, is taking place there. I am grateful to the members of the Reading and South London close reading groups, the Sewing Circle and the Quilting B, particularly those members of the Sewing Circle who took part in the session on *Lone Star* in December 1998. Thank you too to Andrew Klevan for discussing *Imitation of Life* and *Lone Star* with me, Iris Luppa for directions on Brecht, Jacob Leigh for his assistance in preparing the illustrations, and Jonathan Bignell for help getting started. My thanks and love are due to Rebecca and to my family for their ongoing inspiration and support. I would also like to thank Yoram Allon and his colleagues at Wallflower Press for the opportunity, and for their patience.

One of the aims of this book is to explore the expressive potential of visual style in the cinema, another to celebrate a tradition of criticism sensitive to mise-en-scène. I would like to acknowledge the accomplishments of the critics who are quoted below, and the extraordinary achievements of the film-makers they write about.

INTRODUCTION

In writing about film, 'mise-en-scène' is sometimes used as a straight-forward descriptive term but it is really a concept, complicated but central to a developed understanding of film. This book begins with a workable definition of the term, but the chapters that follow are designed to explore the more complex aspects of the concept. By the end of the book, I hope that the different nuances of mise-en-scène will have been made clear, but along the way — such is the importance of mise-en-scène — we will have encountered a whole range of ideas concerned with the way films work and the methods which critics have developed to understand them.

Thinking and writing of mise-en-scène — which is concerned with visual style in the cinema — helped the study of film achieve maturity. Yet many textbooks of today, including those which aim to give an introduction to the subject area, underestimate the importance of mise-en-scène. Some writers offer inadequate or even incorrect definitions of the term, while others seem unaware of the full implications of visual style.

There is, however, some superb writing which is alive to the impor-tance of mise-en-scène and sensitive to the complexities of film style. The introductions to film studies may not point you in its direction, and some of the articles may only be found in discontinued journals or copyright libraries, but a fine tradition of material nevertheless exists.

An important role of this book, therefore, is identifying approaches that have already been developed and employed. My task is less about saying something new, and more one of bringing together in the same place, some of the ways in which mise-en-scène has been thought about and put to use.

In fact, I have made a deliberate strategy of quoting from the work of other critics, and I have not quoted from any articles I do not consider to be excellent and worth pursuing. This strategy of drawing attention to existing style-based criticism is consolidated in the Appendix, which aims to guide the reader in the direction of the best writing in the field.

Chapter 1 introduces a working definition of mise-en-scène and, making use of a range of quotations, explores the expressive potential of its constituent parts. The emphasis of Chapter 2 is on the integration of different elements of mise-en-scène, how they work in conjunction. It takes a sequence from *Lone Star* (John Sayles, 1996) as an extended example. Chapter 3 examines ideas of integration and coherence at greater length, and discusses some of the problems that arise when elements are not considered in relationship. Chapter 4 looks at the history of mise-en-scène within the development of serious film criticism, which helps to explain a number of the ideas that are bound up in the term. Two particular areas which are explored are the traditional associations of mise-en-scène with popular cinema and with ideas of authorship. Chapter 5 continues this historical thrust in its investigation of ways in which critics have explored visual style, but with a particular emphasis on the mise-en-scène of Hollywood melodrama. Chapter 6 is a case study, which examines strategies employed in the melodrama *Imitation of Life* (Douglas Sirk, 1959), and demonstrates in practice some of the approaches discussed in previous chapters. After the Conclusion, which reflects on the ongoing importance of sensitivity to film style, comes the Appendix, an extensive annotated reading list that identifies some of the best writing on film style and mise-en-scène.

I hope this book will be useful to students of film, on practical courses as well as critical/theoretical courses, and to the film enthusiast at large.

In the introduction to her recent volume of criticism, the novelist A.S. Byatt writes of her belief in 'teaching good reading as the best way of encouraging, and making possible, good writing' (2000: 1). I am not qualified to say whether she is correct about creative writing, and I am less sure that the same thing might be true of film, given the range of creative, practical and technical skills that a film-maker needs to develop. However, I do believe that good viewing is an essential part of making possible good film-making. An appreciation of what is possible is partly dependent on a true recognition of what has already been achieved, and a sense of how style relates to meaning is fundamental to film-making and film viewing alike.

This is a book about the different visual forms through and with which film-makers have worked expressively, but it is also a book about criticism, and the techniques that writers have developed to elucidate and celebrate those accomplishments.

A note on spelling

Personally, I favour the version of mise-en-scène with hyphens and without italicisation, as it appears in the *Oxford English Dictionary*. However 'mise-en-scène' is spelt in different ways by different critics. In French it appears without hyphens, and a number of writers and translators whom I have quoted employ this version, sometimes italicising the word to indicate its etymology. In every case of quotation I have respected the spelling of the original, so do not be surprised to come across several different versions in the course of the book.

1   THE ELEMENTS OF MISE-EN-SCÈNE

A Workable Definition

'Mise-en-scène' is used in film studies in the discussion of visual style. The word is from the French, although it has been employed in English since at least 1833, and has its origins in the theatre. Literally translated it means 'to put on stage', but figurative uses of the term have a long history. For the student of film, a useful definition might be: 'the contents of the frame and the way that they are organised'. Both halves of this formulation are significant — the contents and their organisation.

What are the contents of the frame? They include lighting, costume, décor, properties, and the actors themselves. The organisation of the contents of the frame encompasses the relationship of the actors to one other and to the décor, but also their relationship to the camera, and thus the audience's view. So in talking about mise-en-scène one is also talking about framing, camera movement, the particular lens employed and other photographic decisions. Mise-en-scène therefore encompasses both what the audience can see, and the way in which we are invited to see it. It refers to many of the major elements of communication in the cinema, and the combinations through which they operate expressively.

The main body of this chapter looks at some of the different elements of mise-en-scène, in order to illustrate the range of creative options available to film-makers and to introduce some of the ways in which critics have found the visual field expressive.

Lighting

When I was an undergraduate, I remember studying a shot in *Notorious* (Alfred Hitchcock, 1946) which makes a great deal of the expressive power of lighting: the long take which begins the second sequence of the film. Alicia Huberman (Ingrid Bergman), whose father has just been convicted of treason against the USA, is conducting a soirée. As she and her drunken guests dance or talk, they are illuminated evenly and unremarkably. However, as the scene progresses, Alicia directs her attention towards a silent guest in the foreground of the image. This man sits with his back to the camera, at the very edge of the light which falls on the others. He says nothing when Alicia accuses him of being a party-crasher, or even when she expresses her admiration for him. We know little about this figure, but we may perhaps have identified the silhouette as belonging to the film's male lead, Cary Grant.

The organisation of light, actors and camera makes possible a series of suggestive readings. Cary Grant's darkened silhouette makes it look as though he was sitting in the row in front of us in the cinema. We join Grant in his observation, we are behind him, we share a similar perspective. Grant is scrutinising the inebriated and incautious Bergman, as are we, but we cannot scrutinise Grant. In retrospect this can be seen as an informing image for the film: Cary Grant's character remains an onlooker for most of the movie, and continues to view Alicia judgementally. He does not speak in this scene — later in the movie he refuses to tell Alicia that he loves her, to an almost sadistic degree. (Andrew Britton goes so far as to call Devlin, Grant's character, 'the most detestable leading man in the American popular cinema' (1983: 8).) By associating our view with that of a character who turns out to be an extraordinarily unpleasant hero — and by doing so in a way that draws attention to our own status as members of an audience — the film opens the possibility of a critique of spectatorship.[1]

FIGURE 1 *Notorious*: Devlin (Cary Grant) in silhouette

Costume

George M. Wilson, the philosopher and film theorist, writes about the creative use of costume in *Rebel Without a Cause* (Nicholas Ray, 1955) in his book *Narration in Light*. Discussing the events that take place after the fatal shooting of Plato (Sal Mineo) outside the Planetarium, Wilson writes:

> Jim reaches down and zips up the red jacket that he had given Plato a few moments before, and Judy replaces a shoe that had fallen from Plato's foot. Echoing the earlier images of the temporary 'family' the three kids had briefly formed, these actions have the look of an attempt by the parents to bundle their children against the cold. The gesture, taken in this way, is pathetic and ironic. Jim's father then bends down and places his jacket on Jim's shoulders. ... With the red jacket born away on Plato and with the adult jacket now worn by Jim, an exchange of 'uniforms' has been effected.

The jacket of rebellion is gone, and, as Jim returns to Judy's side, he wears the token of his new and more acceptable status. (1983: 187)

A further detail, not mentioned by Wilson but entirely in keeping with the sense he makes of the scene, is the physical resemblance between Judy (Natalie Wood) and Jim's mother (Ann Doran). As Jim (James Dean) introduces Judy to his parents the two couples are framed separately but symmetrically and, if we have not noticed the similarity before, the correspondence of hairstyle and colour of dress is strikingly apparent (Judy no longer wears her distinctive green sweater, nor the red coat *she* wore in the film's opening sequence). In these ways, the film suggests that Jim and Judy are being subsumed into the world of adult society and, more chillingly, being transformed into younger versions of Jim's parents — a bleak prospect given all that has come before. Only Plato, in Wilson's words, is 'the truly intransigent rebel'.

Colour

Wilson's reading of the jackets partly depends on his sense that the film is drawing one of the familiar cultural associations with the colour red, 'its traditional association with rebellion' (1983: 187). Colour is an important expressive element for film-makers, and is often mobilised by means of costume, which has the advantage of a direct association with a particular character. It might equally, however, be a feature of the lighting, the set decoration, or particular props. Richard Dyer has written about the use of colour in *Home from the Hill* (Vincente Minnelli, 1959):

The film revolves around a conflict between a man (Robert Mitchum) and his wife (Eleanor Parker). The husband's den in the film is painted a deep, blood red all over and is furnished in a 'masculine' way, with leather armchairs, rifles and hunting trophies. The rest of the house is the woman's domain — it is decorated in off-white, with chintzy patterns and in upper-class good taste; she wears pastel colours that blend in with the setting. The house is thus divided dramatically between the male and female parts, as is the family itself. The use of colour, however, goes beyond this, through the way it relates to a blood symbolism that runs through the film. He is associated with blood, with hunting, with death, whereas she is aloof from this, cold and bloodless. Their son (George Hamilton) has to choose between these two sets of values and life-styles. The blood connection goes further still, to subconscious associations of blood — and fear — with maleness and femaleness. Thus Mitchum's room is engorged with blood, as an erect penis, whereas Parker's domain is drained of blood as in menstruation. (1981: 1154–5).

Often elements of mise-en-scène will work, as is the case with the 'blood symbolism' here, in patterns developed across the length of a film.

Props

Andrew Klevan has written about such a process of patterning in *Late Spring* (Yasujiro Ozu, 1949), where he argues that particular household objects in the film 'collect meanings through repeated usage, and develop associations throughout the narrative' (2000: 146). *Late Spring* is a film about a young woman, Noriko (Setsuko Hara), who lives happily with her father Somiya (Chishu Ryu) but who is eventually encouraged, rather against her will, to marry and leave the home which father and daughter had shared. Klevan argues that 'Noriko and Somiya's particular interaction with domestic objects delineates their emotional progression':

Noriko's bentwood chairs, for example, are first seen in her room where Aya and Noriko sit and chat; unlike Somiya, both Aya and Noriko seem to prefer not to sit on the floor. At the start of the film, therefore, it might be claimed that the chairs carry a straightforward meaning: they represent the 'modernity' of the two women because they are a Western style of furniture.

Any emotional resonance gained by the presence of the chairs, however, is achieved by their development within the narrative situations. On both occasions when she is followed up into her room, Noriko settles into her chair with her back towards Somiya and her aunt. The chairs are the furniture to which she flees for comfort and protection, but are also where she ends up appearing confined.

At the end of the film, after Noriko has married, the film returns to her father left alone in the house:

Now the sadness which Somiya feels can be expressed through the use of Noriko's chairs: his sitting on one of the chairs both recalls her absence and conveys an unfamiliar position for him. Thus, a household chair, never pushed to the centre of attention, always deployed or relocated without emphasis, is able to encapsulate both Somiya's loss and the disruption for him in these final moments. (2000: 146–7)

Décor

V.F. Perkins' 'Moments of Choice', an article which should be much better known than it is (see Appendix, for details), examines the range of areas of decision-making involved in film direction, and provides a series of examples of the ways different elements of mise-en-scène (although the word is not used) can be employed expressively. As an example of décor, Perkins turns to Jean Renoir's much admired film, *La Règle du Jeu* (1939):

A justly famous scene in *La Règle du Jeu* … gains much of its effect from Renoir's use of decor. At the start of a country-house party, the aristocratic hostess, Christine, is obliged to confront the gossip surrounding her relationship with a young aviator, André Jurieu. She does this by introducing him to her other guests as a group with a

FIGURE 2 *La Règle du Jeu*: Christine (Nora Gregor), Octave (Jean Renoir) and André (Roland Toutain) hesitate in 'the wings' before making their entrance

speech in praise of pure friendship. The scene is set in the château's entrance hall and the decor is a perfectly credible arrangement of doors, pillars and open space. But Renoir's disposition of his actors and camera turns the space into a theatrical arena as Christine takes André 'centre stage' to present him to the others, grouped at a little distance to constitute the audience, while her husband and his friend look on anxiously and at last proudly from 'the wings'. The sense of Christine's performance as one governed by strict rules, where a wrong move threatens disaster, emerges from another parallel that the decor permits: the camera sees the floor, with Christine and André moving across its black-and-white marble tiles, as a chess-board. The power of the scene largely derives from the tension between Christine's nervously awkward sincerity and the demand implied by the theatre/chess-game image for the precise execution of a delicate manoeuvre. (1981: 1143)

FIGURE 3 Christine speaks to André and the other guests while her husband (Marcel Dalio) and Octave (partly obscured) 'look on anxiously'

Action and performance

At an important base level, mise-en-scène is concerned with the action and the significance it might have. Whilst thinking about décor, lighting and the use of colour, we should not forget how much can be expressed through the direction of action and through skillful performance. A very great deal of significance can be bound up in the way in which a line is delivered, or where an actor is looking at a particular moment. The effects that Perkins attributes to Renoir's film are in part suggested by the performances, and would not be possible without them.

Critics have often found writing about performance and the complexities it can suggest very difficult, but this should not lead one to overlook the extent to which performance is central to our understanding of narrative film, nor the work of writers who have managed to describe and interpret performance sensitively. One of the best examples of such writing might be the account of two moments of Barbara Bel Geddes' performance in *Caught* (Max Ophuls, 1949), described and interpreted by V.F.

Perkins in his article 'Must We Say What They Mean?' (1990b). As an example for this discussion, I have also tried to capture a moment from Ophuls' film and Bel Geddes' performance.

Modelling a mink coat in a department store, Maud (or Leonora as she now calls herself) is addressed by a curious man leaning against the perfume counter (Curt Bois). He clicks his fingers and beckons her over, gesturing to a piece of jewelry in his hand: 'You like it, darling? Oh, I hope you're not offended because I call everybody darling. What a charming coat! May I see the lining?' Leonora is immediately distrustful of this man (who later reveals himself to be Franzi Kartos, personal representative of the industrialist Smith Ohlrig), but mindful of the relations between customer and employee she accedes to his request.

'Only forty-nine ninety-five, plus tax' Leonora states, opening the coat one side at a time. The manner in which she opens each half of the coat is by holding the edge and pulling back the material with a quick move-ment of her forearm. Leonora opens one half of the coat as she reveals the price. She lets a beat pass before opening the second half, on the line 'plus tax'. Once the coat is open, revealing the evening gown which she wears underneath, she holds the pose for a second. The whole time she stares Franzi in the eye, challenging him to meet her gaze rather than to look down at her body. At the end of the exchange she wraps the coat tightly around herself.

In contrast to a moment before, when two women had examined the coat and paid not the slightest attention to the person wearing it, Leonora now finds herself in the opposite situation: Franzi, who is collecting young women to attend a rich man's party on Ohlrig's yacht, has no interest in the coat at all. Leonora's leveled gaze, and her parodic suggestion of 'flashing', of exposing herself, convey her awareness of, and her contempt for, Franzi's motives. The look into his eye and the sardonic tone of her voice suggest a challenge in her actions, defiance despite her obli-gation to model the coat. Moreover, by her juxtaposition of the price with the staggered revelation of her body (the pacing of this action also suggesting a strip-tease) she indicates to us and to Franzi the base level of the suggested transaction — the whole activity is not very far from

FIGURE 4 *Caught*: ' ... plus tax'

prostitution, with Franzi as pimp or sexual procurer. *Caught* is a film in which the *partial* awareness of the protagonist is very important. What is skilful here is the way in which Bel Geddes suggests Maud's very clear understanding of Franzi's proposition, and what she thinks of it, even if she is unable to perceive the ironic relationship of this situation to her earlier fantasy of meeting a handsome young millionaire.

As an example of the potential complexity that the smallest performance decision can generate, consider a moment from the performance of Martin Landau as Leonard in *North by Northwest* (Alfred Hitchcock, 1959), a moment contained within a single shot from the auction scene. Roger Thornhill (Cary Grant) has just discovered the woman he has fallen in love with, Eve Kendall (Eva Marie Saint), in the company of the man who, for reasons yet unclear, is trying to kill him. At the same time, Thornhill's behaviour is beginning to suggest to Phillip Vandamm (James Mason) that Eve is more involved with Thornhill than he had thought. Eve herself, meanwhile, is trying desperately to disguise her emotions. Leonard is placed a little apart from the others, half facing the confrontation between Vandamm, his superior, and Thornhill which takes place over the seated Eve. The shot in question is a medium close up of Leonard, lasting for perhaps two seconds, which interrupts the pattern of reverse field cutting between shots favouring Vandamm and those favouring Thornhill.

Leonard keeps his head completely still and simply looks from Thornhill to Vandamm to Eve — this is where Leonard looks at least, Landau merely looks offscreen. He considers each for a measured period of time, and re-fixes his gaze precisely and abruptly. There is nothing hesitant about the way in which he moves his eyes, it is calm and deliberate, and his eyes travel without pause to their new position. In contrast Vandamm, in the various views we are given of him, blinks, moves his head, and plays with his glasses as he begins to question the nature of Eve's feelings (his hesitancy also indicated by the way in which he removes his hand from her neck where it had affectionately but possessively rested). Despite the wittiness of his exchange with Thornhill, Vandamm is disturbed to the extent that he almost forgets to place his bid.

This small still element of Landau's performance has a number of effects. Firstly, the shape drawn with his eyes helps the audience to trace the emotional triangle played out in the scene — reinforced elsewhere in the sequence by compositions that play with the group of three, and which tend to exclude Leonard. Secondly, it indicates Leonard's own pattern of thoughts — a growing need to re-evaluate his understanding of the Vandamm/Eve/Thornhill relationship. Thirdly, it reveals aspects of Leonard's character. There is something cold and emotionally removed about his way of looking. By keeping his head still and only moving the eyes, he suggests an extreme level headedness. By only looking where he has to, and without extraneous effort, he conveys incisive efficiency. Fourthly, Vandamm is equally the object of this gaze. This, combined with the way that Leonard is removed from the others, suggests not only his distance from the emotional struggle, but also indicates the beginning of Leonard's differing perspective on events from that of his emotionally involved superior.

FIGURE 5 *North by Northwest:* Martin Landau as Leonard

FIGURE 6

FIGURE 7

FIGURE 8 *North by Northwest*: The emotional triangle

Space

This might not immediately strike us as one of the contents of the frame (or as belonging to the same order of existence as the other items on this list) but space is a vital expressive element at a film-maker's disposal. In thinking about space we might include the personal space between performers and our sense of when it is impinged upon, but also 'blocking', that is, the relationships expressed and patterns created in the positioning of the actors. Consider again Perkins' understanding of the arrival scene from *La Règle du Jeu*: it is 'Renoir's disposition of his actors and camera' that 'turns the space into a theatrical arena' and makes much of the scene's metaphorical power available to the audience. Similarly, the meanings suggested in the scene from *Notorious* are as dependent on the organisation of actors and camera as they are on the lighting.

Groups of three characters give a particular range of opportunities for expressing relationships in these terms. In the article 'Movies and Point of View', Douglas Pye discusses the ways in which the blocking of three

FIGURE 9 *The Lusty Men*: Wes (Arthur Kennedy), Louise (Susan Hayward) and Jeff (Robert Mitchum)

characters in *The Lusty Men* (Nicholas Ray, 1952) creates 'conflicting 2:1 groupings that are central to the film's narrative and its themes' (2000: 30). As the article reveals, groups of three characters can be organised in particularly interesting ways because the spectator can view the configuration both across the image, or in depth. Pye's analysis draws attention to the ways the blocking helps dramatise a complex struggle for one character's allegiances between two individuals and the ways of life they represent.

The Position of the Camera

In thinking about space we have begun, if we had not before, to think about the *organisation* of the contents of the frame. Moreover, in considering space we have also begun implicitly to think about the position of the camera. If we say, with Pye, that 'Louise is seen in the background of the shot but visually between Wes and Jeff, while in terms of the position of the characters in the rooms, Jeff is also between Wes and Louise' (2000: 30), it should be clear that at least the first of these observations presupposes a particular viewpoint on the characters.

Importantly, the position of the camera governs our access to the action. How we experience a given set of events is going to be profoundly affected by the nature of the view, or views, with which we are presented. Take, as a hypothetical example, a scene involving two figures talking as they walk along a river bank. It would be possible to film the event in long shot, perhaps from the other side of the river. This would literally, and perhaps emotionally, hold the audience at a certain distance. Or, one could track along in front of the characters giving the spectator an intimate and equal view of each. Or, one could have the camera tracking slightly to one side, thus favouring one of the characters because we are closer to the actor and can study her or his facial expressions with greater ease. Or, one could shoot the sequence in a series of shots which alternate between a view of a character looking offscreen and a series of shots representing her optical point of view. A tracking point of view figure — other things being equal — is likely to encourage the audience to empathise with a character.[2]

The point here is that the position of the camera is going to determine our understanding of the scene. It will, for example, profoundly affect the way we experience a performance. It is one of the most important means by which the nature of our relationship to the characters is defined. Even decisions such as whether we follow a character who 'leads' the camera, or whether the camera has anticipated her or his arrival can subtly shape the relationship the audience has with character and story. In 'Movies and Point of View', Pye discusses the way in which Robert Mitchum's character, Jeff, is considered by the camera in early sequences of *The Lusty Men*:

> For instance, as Jeff leaves the arena, our view remains relatively distant. When the truck drops him, rather than being inside it with Jeff, we are already, as it were, waiting for him; as he breasts the rise, we are in front of him and watch as he walks towards us. We are consistently placed in a way that separates us physically

and allows us to observe. However, this tendency to create spatial and temporal positions for us that are distinct from those of the characters — here positions that to an extent distance us physically from Jeff — is accompanied by other spatial strategies in which at times we see Jeff in mid-shot and close up and even, when he is riding the bull, share his visual experience by means of point of view shots. In the early sequences, then, there is already a tension … between closeness and distance that might in turn imply an interplay between sympathy and scrutiny. (2000: 27)

Film-makers making consistent choices in this area can even determine the nature and tone of a film. In *Personal Views*, a book of great interest to anyone concerned with the interpretation of film style, Robin Wood compares the use of tracking shots characteristic to the work of three directors in order to demonstrate style's role in 'defining [the] relationship between the spectator and the characters'.

Since *Rebecca* (his first American film), one of the instantly iden- tifiable characteristics of Hitchcock's *mise-en-scène* has been the *subjective* tracking shot, that places us in the actor's position and gives us the sensation of moving with him; this usually alternating with backward tracking-shots of the actor moving. The device is a logical extension of the Hitchcockian principle of audience-identifi- cation, an expression of his desire to 'put the audience through it'. In the 'classical' Preminger films of the 'forties and 'fifties, camera- movement has an opposite function, which can be briefly illustrated from *Laura*. Consider the famous sequence leading up to Laura's return — Mark McPherson's obsessive exploration of her apartment and personal belongings, his growing infatuation with a woman who is supposed to be dead. Here a subject that might well have attracted Hitchcock (think of *Vertigo*) is treated in a manner very different. … The camera in *Laura* moves to *watch* the character rather than to implicate us in his movements; having followed McPherson's tour of the living room it not only stops to survey his progress to the

FIGURE 10 *Laura*: The intrusive chairback

next room in detached long-shot, it drops slightly so that a chair-back intrudes into the foreground of the frame. That chairback has nothing of the graceful ornamental function of intervening objects in Ophuls; it is there simply to keep us at our distance. Ophuls's camera has a much stronger tendency to move *with* the characters, beside them and at their pace (in *Madame de...*, to waltz with them); though this is continually offset by intrusions into the frame, by the variability of camera-distance, by the (less frequent, but not uncommon) transference of our attention to other characters or other groups. Equally removed from the audience-participation techniques of Hitchcock and the clinical objectivity and detachment of Preminger, Ophuls's camera-work achieves a perfect balance — in terms of the spectator's involvement — between sympathy and detachment. The sense of closeness without identification is essen-tial to Ophuls' cinema: it is an aspect of that constant delicate intermingling of tenderness and irony that characterizes the Ophuls 'tone'. (1976: 125–6)

Gilberto Perez ascribes a similar epistemological weight to the role and placement of the camera in his discussion of films directed by, and starring, Buster Keaton. Perez argues that the use of the camera places the audience in a similar position to Keaton's characters, in terms of their limitations in the face of an impersonal world. One example that Perez writes about is the moment in *The General* (Buster Keaton and Clyde Bruckman, 1927) when Keaton's Johnnie Grey is so involved in chopping wood to stoke the steam engine he is single-handedly driving that he fails to notice that he has passed through his own and the enemy lines:

> When he eventually looks up from his task and at the enemy troops around him, it's not behind him, where we've been watching the military movements, that he looks first: he stares before him instead, where, as a shot from his point of view now reveals, there are troops too. We may have thought we had a commanding view of the situation, but now we recognize that there was a whole other side we had not previously seen, a side that had been hidden behind the camera just as the troops within our view were hidden behind Buster's back. There were, so to speak, troops behind our backs too. ... Although his surprise is of course greater, his moment of discovery coincides with ours, and he finds out something that we didn't already know. If his perspective is limited, so also, we're not allowed to forget, is ours. (1998: 112)[3]

Framing

The restricted view of Keaton's characters, and its relationship to our own limitations, can also be observed in the use of framing in three shots from the finale of *One Week* (Buster Keaton and Edward F. Cline, 1920). Keaton and his recently-married wife (Sybil Seely) have got their new, although by this time rather damaged, home stuck whilst towing it

FIGURE 11 *The General*

from one side of the railway tracks to the other. In a long shot composed in depth, we watch the couple, the house and the advance of the train. They frantically try to shift the house by hand as we watch the train rush closer. Realising that nothing can be done, they run clear and turn their backs to the line. Keaton covers his eyes. After an agonising approach the train roars past the house on a second track, the existence of which we and the characters were unaware. After a moment's pause, we cut in to a closer shot in which the couple open their eyes, turn and discover their house still standing. Relaxing, they return to arguing. In the third shot, wider than the second but perpendicular to the railway line, a second train travelling in the opposite direction abruptly enters the frame and crashes through the house.

During the three shots we experience the kind of relationship between camera, audience and character to which Perez refers. Firstly, we, like the couple, assume the train is going to hit, our view of its advance creating a sense of anticipation equivalent to that of the characters (and even generating additional suspense — as they frantically work

FIGURE 12 *One week*

FIGURE 13

FIGURE 14

FIGURE 15

the house obscures their view, while we can see the train's approach). When the train misses we realise that we, like they, have come to the wrong conclusion. In the third shot our, and the characters', new sense of events is revealed to be equally misplaced as the second train enters the frame without warning and surprises all of us.

With this gag, Keaton reminds us that what is in the frame is only a selective view of a wider fictional world, and that the act of framing an action presents the film-maker with a whole range of choices including those concerning what is revealed and withheld from the audience.

The interaction of elements

Examining the different aspects of mise-en-scène reveals how many variables there are at the film-makers' disposal, and gives us a sense of how variously expressive they can be. However, as you will already have noticed, each of the examples we have looked at depends for its effect on a combination of elements. In the moment from *La Règle du Jeu* performance ('Christine's nervously awkward sincerity'), décor, camera position and camera movement are all involved — although not clear from the passage quoted from Perkins, it is a movement of the camera which initially draws our attention to the pillar which forms one side of Renoir's metaphorical proscenium arch. Similarly, even the simplest examples we have considered involve taking account of several factors.

It is important to be able to describe the individual elements of mise-en-scène, and it is important to consider each element's potential for expression. But it is worth remembering from the outset that these elements are most productively thought of in terms of their *interaction* rather than individually — in practice, it is the interplay of elements that is significant. Additionally, we need to consider the significance acquired by the individual element by virtue of *context*: the narrative situation, the 'world' of the film, the accumulating strategies that the film-maker adopts. Chapters 2 and 3 consider these areas in greater detail.

2 THE INTERACTION OF ELEMENTS

One of the points which emerged forcefully in Chapter 1 is that it is the interaction of different aspects of mise-en-scène which enables film-makers to accomplish the most interesting effects. Chapter 2 explores an extended example from the 1996 film *Lone Star* in order to develop this sense of interaction at greater length.

Lone Star is a border film. This is a tradition of films — to call it a 'genre' would be to exaggerate the case, and the term 'cycle' suggests a temporal proximity which the films (and works in other media) do not possess — which are set on the US/Mexico border. Perhaps the most famous border film is *Touch of Evil* (Orson Welles, 1958), in which another law enforcement officer works outside his jurisdiction. Typically, border films are concerned with various different kinds of borders, not simply national boundaries, and the degree of difficulty which is involved in crossing them.[1]

The sequence I want to examine takes place just beyond the film's halfway point. Sheriff Sam Deeds (Chris Cooper), in the course of his investigation into the circumstances surrounding the death of Sheriff Wade, takes a trip across the border into Mexico to interview Chucho Montoya (Tony Amendola). Sam asks questions of Chucho. They discuss the extent of his business empire (or rather his kingdom — Chucho is known as El Rey de las Llantas, King of the Tires). In less than specific terms, Chucho responds to Sam's questions about his period of work in Texas, his subsequent return, and business career. Sam's main enquiry provokes an emotional discussion and the scene culminates in the graphic and disturbing flashback which shows the murder of Eladio Cruz (Gilbert R. Cuellar Jr) by Sheriff Wade (Kris Kristofferson).

The sequence begins with a young man removing a tire from a wheel, at the rear of the Llanteria. Sam and Chucho appear through a doorway already talking. Chucho holds a bottle of *CocaCola*. He encourages his employee to take a break, and continues to walk and converse with Sam.

Chucho: Down here, we don't throw everything away like you gringos do.
They emerge from the building.
Recycling, right? We invented that. The government doesn't have to tell people to do it.
Sam: You own this place, huh?
Chucho: This place, the one across the street, three or four others in Ciudad León. Soy el Rey de las Llantas! King of the Tires.
Chucho stops and turns to face Sam.
A lot of your people rolling over that bridge on my rubber.
Sam: So you lived in the States for a while?
Chucho: Fifteen years.

FIGURE 16 *Lone Star*

FIGURE 17

FIGURE 18

FIGURE 19

Sam: Made some money, came back here.

Chucho: Something like that.

Sam: D'you ever know a fellow named Eladio Cruz?

A pause. Chucho looks away, and then looks back at Sam.

Chucho: You're the sheriff of Rio county, right? Un jefe muy respetado.

Chucho draws a line in the dirt between the two men with the bottle which he plants at its end. He stands up and beckons to Sam.

Step across this line.

Sam walks away from Chucho, parallel to the line rather than crossing it.

Ay, qué milagro! You're not the sheriff of nothing anymore. Just some tejano with a lot of questions I don't have to answer. ... A bird flying south, you think he sees this line? Rattlesnake, javelina? Whatever you got. You think halfway across that line they start thinking different? Why should a man?

Sam: Your government has always been pretty happy to have that line, the question's just been where to draw it.

Chucho walks parallel to the line until he is opposite Sam, then turns to face him again.

Chucho: My government can go fuck itself, and so can yours. I'm talking about people here! Men! ... Mi amigo, Eladio Cruz is giving some friends of his a lift one day in the back of his camión, but because they're on one side of this invisible line and not the other, they've got to hide in the back como criminales, and because over there he's just another Mex bracero, any man with a badge is his jefe. *As Chucho tells his story the camera pans to the left, leaving the present day characters behind, and revealing a broken-down truck stranded on a bridge on a quiet road near the border.*

The central action of the sequence is the line that Chucho draws in the dirt. In drawing the line he is marking a difference between the two individuals, it is an act of separation on a personal scale. Yet it simultaneously refers to the national border, as Chucho's remarks make plain.

In asking Sam to step across the line, Chucho's act becomes a challenge. There is something of throwing down the gauntlet in this moment. When in 1527 Francisco Pizarro, the conquistador, challenged his companions to persevere with their South American expedition, he invited them to step across a line he drew in the sand (Hemming 1983: 26). The action is also a little reminiscent of the kinds of ritualised stand-off that are familiar from Westerns or, closer to home, some of the provocations of Sheriff Wade witnessed earlier in the film, around the pouring and spilling of drinks, or in the confrontation between Wade and Buddy Deeds (Matthew McConaughey). What is certain is that one cannot imagine the late Sheriff Wade walking away from this confrontation in the way that Sam chooses to do. The line could barely be more insubstantial, as Chucho observes, and yet it already possesses a consequence that is almost tangible. It is one boundary among many, in a film in which borders are both insubstantial and yet difficult to cross.

The act of drawing the line is eloquent and effective, but some of the other decisions made by Sayles and his collaborators inflect, develop and enhance the significance of the confrontation.

The cola bottle

Economics, and their relationship to the Texas/Mexico border, are important concerns of the film. The transport of illegal immigrants and the associated privation and exploitation are everywhere to be seen. Earlier in the film characters remark on the sweatshops of Ciudad León and Sam suggests that the American town of Frontera's main tourist attraction is the opportunity for low-budget sex tourism that its proximity to Mexico provides. In this scene, the economic differences that the border helps to sustain are also inescapable — from the discussion about recycling tires to the circumstances in which Eladio was murdered. In this context, the decision to have Chucho use a *CocaCola* bottle to draw his boundary is not a flattering product placement, in fact quite the contrary. Given that the economic and exploitative nature of the relationship between America and its neighbours is very much the subject of attention, to use the clearest symbol of American global economic dominance as a marker is eloquent. It is the governments, Chucho argues, which have drawn these lines in the desert. It is the imperatives of multinational companies, the film suggests, that guide the hand of government policy.[2] And it is the people, like Eladio Cruz, who are the victims of these boundaries and their exploitation.

The uniform

Sam has removed his badge prior to crossing the border, and made the journey in his own car (in contrast, for example, to his first appearance in the film), but he is still wearing the rest of his sheriff's uniform, a uniform which brings with it a weight of association. These associations are felt by both characters and audience. We may again be put in mind of the Western. The film goes out of its way to point up similarities between the dress, and role, of the latter-day sheriff and the traditional figure of Western lore, most prominently in Hollis' (Clifton James) retelling of the night when Buddy Deeds ran Sheriff Charlie Wade out of town.

It is these two previous wearers of the uniform whom Chucho and Sam are most likely to be put in mind of. Sam is continually conscious of the difficulty of filling his father's footsteps, a man in whose shadow and by whose laws he has always had to live — as many of his investigative conversations make clear ('Sheriff Deeds is dead honey, you just Sheriff Junior').

But in this particular encounter our sense, and Chucho's sense, of the relationship between Sam and Charlie Wade is much more active. For Chucho, the uniform of a Rio County Sheriff must powerfully bring him back to his terrible first encounter with North American authority, an authority which Sam inevitably embodies. This connection is dynamically strengthened by the shot that ends the ensuing flashback, when the camera cranes up from Chucho's youthful self hiding for his life under the bridge and, rather than Sheriff Wade's widespread arms upon the parapet, we encounter Sam surveying the scene from the bridge in the present day.

FIGURE 20 *Lone Star*: Buddy Deeds (Mathew McConaughey) confronts Charlie Wade

Casting

In addition to the expressive skills which a performer brings to a film, the casting of a role has consequences for our understanding. It is to take nothing away from Cooper's sensitive performance to suggest that his pasty physiognomy is not of the kind we associate with hero or male lead. (On the contrary, it is one of the pleasures of the film that Sam is not played by someone with the appearance or obvious charisma of a star.) It is one of the film's intelligent decisions, and one that only takes on its full weight in relation to the casting of Sheriffs Wade and Buddy Deeds. In contrast to Cooper, Kristofferson is an iconic figure, and an iconic figure of the past. He brings not only the weight of a star to the role, but also the aura of Peckinpah's Billy the Kid, a whiff of the decay of both the old west and, perhaps, the western genre. And, though not a star at this point of his career, who could appear more clean-shaven or firm-jawed than Matthew McConaughey in the role of Buddy Deeds? Sam's predicament — the impossible task of living up to the past and the legend that was his father — is underlined by the casting.

Claims for the complexity and significance of this scene are not solely dependent on the action and the associations of clothing and bottle, but also the way in which the action has been organised for, and with, the camera. Mise-en-scène does not just describe the contents of the frame, but simultaneously the organisation of those elements. In order to do this we need to have a rather more detailed account of the sequence, one which describes the action in relation to the different shots by which the scene is realised.

It begins with a shot which, at forty-five seconds, is by a considerable margin the longest take of the sequence. The camera tracks left past Chucho's employee at work and meets the two men as they emerge into the open air. The camera accompanies them to the right as they walk together, facing, by and large, the same direction, Chucho leading the way. When, however, Chucho says, 'A lot of your people [are] rolling over that bridge on my rubber,' he turns to face Sam, making for a more confrontational relationship. Despite referring to the extent to which citizens of the United States use Mexican remolds, the tenor of the sentence discriminates rather than insists on things in common — 'your' and 'my' actually work to accentuate the difference rather than illustrate the point of contact.

As Sam asks his next question ('So you lived in the States for a while?') the long take ends and the scene continues in shorter shots, cut in a reverse field pattern. Both men remain in the frame from the waist up, but we view one from over the other's shoulder. This arrangement continues for several shots until the point at which Chucho bends to draw the line in the dirt, when he disappears from the bottom of the frame, leaving Sam alone for a moment.

The film cuts to show Chucho drawing the line in the dirt between the positions where he and Sam stand, but when Chucho straightens and steps back the camera follows, excluding Sam from the frame. We are then presented with a view of Sam which registers his response to Chucho's actions. For a fleeting moment both men are in shot together, but then Sam starts off parallel to the line and Chucho is left behind. From this point onwards we never see the two in the same frame again. The pair continue to converse in reverse angle, but each character is removed completely from shots of the other.

FIGURE 21 Charlie Wade (Kris Kristofferson)

FIGURE 22 Sam Deeds (Chris Cooper)

In discussing the famous long takes of *Touch of Evil*, that earlier border film, Robin Wood has written that 'camera movement connects, editing separates'. This is a useful rule of thumb, which is worth bringing to mind on any occasion when confronted by long takes or camera movement; although it is essential to bear in mind Wood's qualification that this, 'like most textbook rules, has some foundation in elementary practice but needs drastic qualification when confronted by the work of a major creative artist' (1976: 143).[3] This sense of connection which the 'textbook rule' illustrates, is partly dependent on a property which one can attribute to any two elements that appear in the same shot, long take or otherwise: a sense of their sharing continuous space and real time. *Lone Star* is a film that plays with this property with intelligence, not least in the film's most characteristic stylistic strategy: the single takes which travel impossibly, by means of camera movement, between the past and the present. These shots cheat our expectation of continuous space and time whilst drawing on the residual sense of connection, by placing events and characters separated by thirty or forty years in the same take. In this way the film suggests, with great economy, the contiguity of past and present, a sense of present happenings being played out in the very same spaces as the events of the past. In *Lone Star* even this border is not easily maintained, and the sense of history acting on present day events is vividly evoked.[4]

The seamlessness of these connections form part of the background of any statement we would wish to make about the découpage of the scene with the bottle. (Découpage is another French term employed in film criticism, which refers to the way in which a scene is broken down into patterns of different shots.) The sense that 'camera movement connects, editing separates' is active in the discriminations between the longer take that begins the sequence and the shorter shots that follow. The related decisions about when the characters are framed together and when they are framed apart also draw upon that sense of connection which belonging to the same frame bestows on different elements.

There is a significant correlation between the degree of conflict which is taking place between the two men and the way in which they are framed. In the first shot, both are framed together; after Chucho has turned to face Sam, and made the remark about Sam's people and his tires, the film cuts between a series of much shorter shots, but both remain on screen in every shot. Once the line has been drawn in the dust, a further act of separation takes place, and the two are framed on their own.

The framing and cutting might be said to be taking its cue from the action — certainly, there is a pertinent relationship between the decisions about how the action on screen has been captured and the nature, flow, and shape of the drama. Perhaps we can even pursue this relationship further by drawing an analogy between the border on the ground and the border of the frame — the separation of the men in terms of on- and off-screen space follows directly from the drawing of the boundary.

At the climax of the scene, after Chucho has walked parallel to the line until he again faces Sam, and while he makes his impassioned plea — 'I'm talking about people here!' — the camera zooms, almost imperceptibly, toward both Sam and Chucho. It is a small movement, and it helps to underline the urgency of what has been said, but it also has the effect of bringing them closer to each other. It is a movement against the drift of the rest of the scene: the parallel edging closer working to emphasise, for the first time in some time, the similarities rather than the differences.

Conclusion

The line is a mere scratch. It is unlikely that the bird flying south would even perceive the line, let alone pay it heed. It is arbitrary, indistinct and yet it holds enormous power. That the line is both a distinction between individuals and a representation of a national border is crucial. On either side are two men caught, like so many of the film's other characters, in an awkward negotiation between personal relationships and public roles and social structures.[5] Two 'people', yet simultaneously the King of the Tires or Sheriff of Rio County. In this, the line is a manifestation of the film's major motif — the border. In *Lone Star* we are shown, and made to feel, borders of race and class and gender and nationality. Borders which are, like this one, simultaneously arbitrary and potent. Or other boundaries, like the one between past and present, which break down only too easily.

There is a whole wealth of material which this account has not touched on at all. So far, we have only examined the action itself in the broadest terms. We have not considered the *way* in which Chucho draws his line, the deliberation with which he puts down the bottle at its end, the texture of the gravel or the effort which is required to make the mark. The details of performance have almost entirely escaped this account: the way, for example, in which Chucho lifts his Coke bottle and looks Sam in the eye, when he says, 'Something like that'. Moreover, it is important to note that this brief account of framing and découpage only describes the general pattern employed in the sequence. We have not examined the decisions that have been made about when to show us Sam's face, and when Chucho's. When are we watching the speaker, and when are we shown the response of the listener?[6] Nor have we contemplated the fact that the camera is already surveying the scene when the characters emerge into view, and questioned whether this affects our relationship to the action in any way. Even regarding the elements of mise-en-scène that we have considered, there are a whole range of artistic choices which are yet to be discussed, and which are of great significance.

Nevertheless, this brief examination has touched on international economics, father-son relationships, race relations, and people reaching out across a political divide. The range of implications, influences, consequences and ideas that an intelligent mise-en-scène can organise, and bring into stimulating relationship, is striking.

3   COHERENT RELATIONSHIPS

Another way of looking at the point with which the last chapter finished, is to observe that in order to make sense of the one moment, we have had to balance a detailed examination of the sequence itself with perspectives derived from an understanding of the rest of the film, knowledge of the traditions and conventions within and with which the film is working (those of the western, for example), and information from the world outside of the film (such as the global standing of the *CocaCola* corporation).

I am particularly interested here in reflecting on the way that my attempts to make sense of the sequence draw extensively from other parts of the film. The persuasiveness of my argument about a number of features (the border motif, the interpretation of single shot against cutting) is substantially dependent on being able to demonstrate that they form part of a consistent pattern of decisions within the film, that they relate to the film's recurrent strategies. Similarly, my understanding of the intricacies of the exchange between the two men is informed by a whole host of perspectives that I bring to the scene, derived from those that precede or follow it. In short, it is terribly difficult to make claims for an individual element or moment without considering it within the context provided by the rest of the film.

Traditionally, debates around artistic coherence have been a way of considering individual techniques in context and in relationship.

Coherence

The idea of coherence has been very important to critics concerned with mise-en-scène, although it is a notion which has a history in the discussion of art which stretches back at least as far as the ancient Greeks (some authorities suggest Aristotle, others Plato), and which has been associated with diverse critical and artistic movements in the intervening period.[1] This paradigm has sometimes been described as organicism, because of its emphasis on an 'organic' relationship between the parts and the whole — that is, the relationship between elements in the admired artwork seems natural and mutually beneficial rather than being too obviously constructed or negatory. The whole formed is greater than the sum of its parts.

In a time-based medium like film, there seem to be two distinct ways in which we can talk about coherence. Firstly, there is coherence across the work. One aspect of this would be the idea of a visual motif — an element which acquires significance through repetition.[2] In the last chapter, I argued that the border was a major motif in *Lone Star*, reappearing with many different variations in a number of sequences in the film. In Chapter 1 the bentwood chairs of *Late Spring*, or the 'blood symbolism' of *Home from the Hill* might be accurately be described as motifs. In each case, the subsequent appearance of the motif brings with it the weight of earlier associations. But coherence across a work would also apply to other aspects of the relationship between one moment and the rest, including consistency of tone and viewpoint, and the qualification that the individual element receives from its context. The context provided by the use of single shots connecting past and present in *Lone Star* helped my claims for the significance of the long take at the beginning of the scene with the bottle, as did the contrast between that shot and rest of the sequence. (Alternatively, a director who chooses to work consistently in long shot may, on breaking this pattern with a significant close up, benefit from the emphasis of the unique departure.)

Secondly, we can talk about coherence between the different elements of a single moment.[3] In the broadest sense, critics have often written about the integration of form and content, that is, the way in which the form of a film articulates, or shapes, its content. Some critics would say the form determines the content, or even that the two cannot be distinguished, that the form *is* the content. In more specific terms, we might talk about the way in which different elements of mise-en-scène, or different areas of decision-making, interact to achieve a significant effect. Returning to my discussion of the relationship between the action and the way it is presented in the sequence from *Lone Star*, it is difficult to see which is leading which: does the camera movement sensitively support the understanding we have arrived at from the action, or is our interpretation of the action dependent on the perspective provided by framing and cutting? Or, indeed, what about all the different elements of mise-en-scène which go to make up 'the action'? The point is that everything is pulling in the same direction: the decisions are integrated in the service of the drama. Criticism sensitive to mise-en-scène is concerned with this synthesis.

For the film-maker trying to achieve expressive significance, or for the critic making a convincing interpretation, the extent to which a coherent pattern can be established is of vital importance. If Perkins can point out that in another scene of *La Règle du Jeu* the characters put on a revue using a pair of pillars to construct a proscenium arch for their stage, it helps to strengthen the persuasiveness of his account of the 'theatrical' nature of the arrival scene. If Richard Dyer can relate the décor of Mitchum's den in *Home from the Hill* to 'the blood symbolism that runs through the film' then the more cogent his argument becomes. If John Sayles can create a sequence, or even a shot, in which the expressive potential of every element of mise-en-scène is organised in a coherent relationship then the richer the film will prove. It is not, ultimately, the individual elements of mise-en-scène that are significant, rather the relationship between elements, their interaction within a shot and across the narrative.

However, as some critics have pointed out, coherence is not the only factor involved. The simplest and least interesting work can, in one sense, be perfectly coherent. Art historian E.H. Gombrich has suggested that 'organic unity' is of itself a fairly small claim. He argues that Raphael's *Madonna della Sedia* is admirable not merely because it has an eloquent and effective form but that it succeeds in these terms whilst also fulfilling the stringent conventions of classical representational painting. In the work, Raphael has found a solution which satisfies 'two mutually limiting demands — that of lifelikeness and that of arrangement' (1966: 74). Similarly, in *Film as Film*, a book deeply concerned with coherence, V.F. Perkins argues that, 'The narrative picture, in most of its forms, submits itself to the twin criteria of order and credibility.' The film-maker's aim, he suggests, 'is to organise the world to the point where it becomes most meaningful but to resist ordering it out of all resemblance to the real world which it attempts to evoke' (1972: 70). Robin Wood, in *Personal Views*, argues that in admiring coherence in a work one is really admiring the existence of coherence *and* complexity: 'The notion of coherence is only meaningful in conjunction with concepts like "complexity", "density", "inner tensions"; it can never be an *absolute* criterion' (1976: 18).

Examining the problems which result when different elements of film style are considered in isolation illustrates some important points about mise-en-scène.

Context and content

One of the problems for a critical approach which does not consider the interaction of elements is that it neglects the shading that a given technique will receive from its context and the content to which it gives form. One element of the orthodoxy of British film criticism in the period before writing sensitive to mise-en-scène developed, was known as the 'Film Appreciation' school of criticism.[4] 'Film Appreciation' is the subheading of one of the school's later but most influential texts, Ernest Lindgren's *The Art of the Film*. As part of his exploration of film technique, Lindgren discusses the different effects than can be achieved by varying the height of the camera. He writes:

If the camera is raised above eye-level so that it looks down on the subject it will produce a picture in which the subject appears dwarfed and of diminished importance; contrariwise, if placed below eye-level and directed upwards, the size and importance of the subject will appear exaggerated. (1948: 122)

Charles Barr was one of a number of critics who found this approach too mechanistic. The 'standard writing about film' of the late 1950s seemed 'brutally' reductive:

Certain things were held up as typical of expressive film-making — Ernest Lindgren has all these examples of the high-angle shot and the low-angle shot. Meaning and experience seem to be defined in such a reductive way with no real scope for complexity of texture and complexity of response.[5]

At the risk of making Lindgren a little unfairly the straw man of the argument, it is important to draw attention to the dangers for the critic in assigning particular effects to specific techniques. This can be demonstrated by returning to V.F. Perkins' 'Moments of Choice', and a passage in which he examines a low angle shot from Nicholas Ray's *The Lusty Men*:

In *The Lusty Men*, Ray introduces his rodeo star hero in a shot which starts with the camera looking in through the gate of a bull-pen. The animal charges along its track to halt at the gate with its eyes glinting in fierce close-up. At this the image tilts upwards to frame Mitchum above the animal, preparing to mount. A direct contrast is drawn between two kinds of strength — the power of a natural force, and the force of human determination. But the camera's movement links these two images in comparison as well as contrast. For all his apparent mastery, as we look up to him outlined against the sky, Robert Mitchum is like the bull in being contained within the structures of the rodeo: his image, too, is framed, hemmed in, by the wooden posts of the bull pen.

FIGURE 23 *The Lusty Men*: 'one of the all time greats'

The movement and angle of the shot give a precisely calculated degree of overstatement to the assertion of mastery. Within fifteen seconds Mitchum will be floundering, injured, in the dirt of the arena. His previous inward smile of self-satisfaction at the commentator's tribute to his prowess, his pose of confident virility as he tightens his belt on the words 'one of the all-time greats', are opened up to irony by the camera's too hearty endorsement of his supremacy. (1981: 1145)

In Perkins' example we can clearly see that the low angle shot, through its context, gives just the opposite effect to the literal impression claimed by Lindgren. The nuances, and the range of effects, that can be provided by the position of the camera are considerable and we cannot simply identify one meaning with one technique. Crucially, as Perkins' account makes clear, the context in which a technique appears, including the content to which it gives form, will contribute to determining its effect.[6]

Ironic overstatement like this is a possibility for the director because the expressiveness of a film style is so much a matter of balance, of what happens when you put together, in a particular way, a posture, a facial expression, an off-screen voice and a camera viewpoint. At the very centre of the director's job is this task of co-ordination. Direction works with the various talents of highly-skilled artists to ensure that their contributions meet in a coherent design. (1981: 1145)

Understanding the interaction of elements prevents one from developing a mechanistic view of the relationship between style and meaning.

Douglas Pye has convincingly argued that even the most customary strategies can become significant through their context. The example he provides is the reverse field cutting through Guy and Bruno's first conversation in *Strangers on a Train* (Alfred Hitchcock, 1951), in which that familiar technique for shooting dialogue becomes a resonant expressive device because of its position within the rest of the film (including the relationship between the characters established by the parallel montage which immediately precedes the scene) and its pertinence to the material it represents.

Thus the use of, for instance, angle/reverse angle cutting with eye-line match in a dialogue sequence may be a mechanical response to the problem of how to film the scene, or a highly self-conscious strategy with a precise and considered place in the systems of the film. ... Hitchcock's use of angle/reverse angle in the initial meeting between Guy and Bruno in *Strangers on a Train* self-consciously draws on the full potential of that familiar strategy to embody simul-taneous and intermeshed parallelism and contrast; but it carries ... that significance only as part of Hitchcock's unfolding formal system of cross-cutting. Only in that network of dramatic, formal and other decisions (contrasting clothes, angles of movement, Guy's acci-dental kick which precipitates the meeting) can the significance and status of the formal decision be weighed. The insistence of

45

FIGURE 24 *Strangers on a Train*: reverse field cutting with eye-line match

FIGURE 25

FIGURE 26 *Strangers on a Train*: Guy Haines (Farley Grainger) and Bruno Anthony (Robert Walker)

FIGURE 27

Hitchcock's paralleling of the characters through angle/reverse angle cutting can even, against Guy's blithe dismissal of Bruno's idiosyncrasy, take on ironic force. (1989: 48)

A number of films from the 1950s employ similarities in the mise-en-scène (and, in this case, editing) to suggest a relationship between ostensibly opposed hero and villain. Peter Lehman and William Luhr have written about the way in which such a strategy in *The Searchers* (John Ford, 1956) works to undermine the apparent opposition between Ethan Edwards (John Wayne) and the white settlers on the one hand and Scar (Henry Brandon) and the Comanches on the other:

Doorways, the openings in Indian tepees, and cave mouths supply the most prominent formal pattern in *The Searchers*. Ford establishes the pattern, in all cases, by placing the camera behind the openings and shooting out at a character or characters. In the nine central shots that establish this pattern, the visible sides of the portals emphasize the interior position of the camera. ... The shot of Ethan framed by the smoking ruins of the doorway points to the ruin of that treasured family unit. ... This pattern reverses in the Indian culture. The shot through the tepee entrance places the spectacle of the village's destruction within the framework of another culture's family units. ... If the tepee frames through which we see Ethan indicate differences in the cultures involved; the establishment of an interior family space stresses an important similarity. (1977: 100–102)

Similarly Ian Cameron, in an important early article on Hitchcock and suspense, points to the way in which '*The Man Who Knew Too Much* [1956], like any other Hitchcock film, is full of linkages between sequences: details which will make the audience, consciously or more often unconsciously, connect one scene or character or action with another' (1963: 8). Such 'linkages' clearly depend on coherence across a work. In common with the motif, to which this strategy is related, the effect relies

FIGURE 28 *The Searchers*

FIGURE 29

FIGURE 30

FIGURE 31

on the audience bringing a previous association to bear — in this case an association caused by graphic similarity. Such structures can also be used to establish forms of dramatic irony. The 'formal pattern' of *The Searchers* provides a perception which is available only to the audience, who are privileged over the characters. It is one of the ways within the film in which a complex parallel is established between two groups of characters who are not inclined to notice it themselves. Mise-en-scène is here touching on potentially complex patterns of point of view.

Mechanics and meaning

If one consequence of the coherent relationship in an artwork is that critic and artist need to consider the qualification or consolidation that a single element receives from those that surround it, then another is that we must equally be aware that a single element may contribute to a range of different outcomes. We cannot simply ascribe one meaning to one technique partly because, in a rich film, one stylistic means can contribute to a range of different semantic ends.

For example, the tilt up in *The Lusty Men* from the head of the bull that reveals Jeff (Mitchum) preparing to mount, contrasts animal strength with human resolve. Yet simultaneously, Perkins argues, the connection of the camera movement also offers a comparison between the two — a suggestion strengthened by the extent to which bull and rider are both constrained by the structure of the bullpen. Were it not for the low angle from which the camera tilts, we would not be able to see the woodwork that fences Jeff in. Moreover, the camera is close enough for us to experience the ferocity of the bull, and to be able to read Jeff's facial expressions: his initial hesitancy and subsequent self-satisfied smile. And, of course, the low angle is central to achieving the 'ironic overstatement' identified by Perkins.

Additionally, the placement and movement of this shot may form part of other patterns within the film — it may, for example, contribute to the balance between 'closeness and distance', 'sympathy and scrutiny' that Pye identifies in the early sequences of the film. Certainly, the tilt up confers and receives significance in relation to Jeff's forthcoming fall 'which leaves us, in contrast to the first low angle shots, looking *down* at Jeff on the ground' (2000: 26). In the integrated film, the individual stylistic element will have consequences for a complex network of meanings.

If the film-maker needs to be aware of the potential range of effects of the individual stylistic choice, then so does the critic. However, a frequent mistake is for a writer to curtail her or his discussion when only a single consequence of a stylistic decision has been identified. Writing about continuity editing seems to suffer particularly from this phenomenon. Once it has been established that a given cut helps create an illusion of continuous space and time, a critic is often satisfied, and fails to discuss any of the other ways in which the timing or nature of that cut might be significant. Yet achieving continuity is just the beginning — in the fully realised film, the effects of a cut may be subtle and various. Whilst montage, or other overtly consequential patterns of editing, are frequently celebrated, there remains a marked tendency to underplay the expressive potential of continuity editing.

An analogous problem can sometimes affect writing about suspense, but Ian Cameron's two articles on Hitchcock and suspense (called 'Hitchcock 1: and the Mechanics of Suspense' and 'Hitchcock 2: Suspense and Meaning') provide a salutary lesson in this respect. Like many a student of film, Cameron wishes to understand the mechanics of suspense. He wants to know how it is that Hitchcock can bring us to the edge of our seats despite our knowledge that the 'clean-limbed hero will make it at the end, and that the hoods are destined for jail or burial — if there is anything left to bury' (1962b: 5). But Cameron also recognises that suspense itself is only a means to an end. Rather than concluding his enquiry at the level of mechanics, he goes on to address the relationship between 'suspense and meaning'. As he writes of the famous Albert Hall sequence in *The Man Who Knew Too Much*:

> By building up to it with this tremendous suspense, Hitchcock gives the maximum importance to Jo's scream. But why should

he place that value on the scream? The deprecatory explanation, which is true, is that the set-up absolutely asks to be turned into a big set-piece. If that were the only reason, one could write the film off. But it is not. (1963: 10)

The article then proceeds to discuss what the sequence's suspense *itself* articulates, and how it makes tangible the film's major themes and concerns. (Robin Wood's introduction to *Hitchcock's Films* (1965) also contains a valuable discussion of how Hitchcock's suspense embodies a range of concerns central to the films in which it appears.)

Perhaps we should leave the last word on this critical point to Stanley Cavell who writes, in the enlarged edition of *The World Viewed*:

Suppose that it would be true to describe what is shown on the screen as a shot of a stairway. This description may or may not have a point (beyond cataloguing the shot). If one calls what is shown a 'point of view shot', one may go on to say that such a shot may be established by, for example, cutting to it from the face of a character and cutting from it back to that face. ... If, however, you go on to say why *this* way of establishing a point of view is used, and why *here*, and why with respect to *this* character, and why by way of *this* content, then you are proposing a critical understanding of this passage. Its interest will depend upon its faithfulness to the intention of this work. But what will you be saying if you say, speaking about this work, that this shot is a point of view shot, and you go on to say nothing further about this shot in this work? Unless your words here are meant to correct a false impression, they do not so much as add up to a remark. They are at most the uttering of a name, which, as Wittgenstein puts it, is a preparation for going on to say something. (1979: 187–8)

Finally, failing to think about elements in their interaction is a problem for the definition of mise-en-scène provided by Bordwell and Thompson in their popular text, *Film Art: An Introduction*. *Film Art* is well worth investigating, not least because it is a good place to learn the terminology for describing mise-en-scène: what 'canting' the camera means, or the difference between a pan and a track. However, it is my belief that the definition of mise-en-scène offered in the book is misleading. Bordwell and Thompson restrict their definition of mise-en-scène to those elements common to film and theatre. The definition of mise-en-scène therefore makes no reference to framing, camera movement or the position of the camera. Instead, *Film Art* devotes a separate chapter (entitled 'Cinematographic Properties') to the discussion of these areas.[7] Further reflection, on both criticism and film-making, reveals the shortcomings of the approach.

Take the example from *Notorious*, where I argued that the mise-en-scène is organised so that it appears as though Cary Grant is sitting in the row of the cinema in front of us. This effect is, as previously discussed, partly dependent on the lighting of the scene, but viewed from another angle, the image which I am claiming to be important would be completely lost. The sense of a spectator's head and shoulders in front of us would no longer be suggested, and seen from elsewhere Cary Grant would be well illuminated. Or, what if we wish to make a claim about the blocking of the actors, like Pye's remarks on *The Lusty Men*? Again, the relationship which we feel significant is not only reliant on the way the actors are standing in relation to each other, but equally the perspective given to us by the camera. Move the camera and the image will change.

Moreover, this sense that any comment about mise-en-scène includes, a priori, the camera's view as well as the action — that the definition of mise-en-scène must include framing, composition — is powerfully confirmed by reference to the physical realities of film-making. On set or location, film-makers do not stage the action and only subsequently think about where the camera is going to be placed in order record it. Similarly, to discuss the lighting of a shot without reference to the position of the camera is to misunderstand how films are made — one does not light the set and then set about deciding where the camera is going to be placed. Rather, a set is lit with the framing and movement of the camera absolutely in mind.

4   INVESTIGATIONS IN THE CRITICAL HISTORY
OF MISE-EN-SCÈNE

This chapter examines a number of examples of the role of mise-en-scène within the history of writing about film. This is a subject of considerable interest of itself — mise-en-scène has played a crucial part in the development of serious film criticism — but it is particularly important to us because a sense of history will enable us to further develop our understanding of what is at stake in the concept of mise-en-scène. The chapter, therefore, does not attempt to give an exhaustive chronology but rather it makes its priority the selection of examples which illustrate the range of ideas in play.

Cahiers and Movie

Although one can quite properly refer to the mise-en-scène of any film, in film criticism mise-en-scène has a particular association with Hollywood cinema. Also, mise-en-scène is intimately connected to arguments about why the director, rather than the scriptwriter, should be considered the artist responsible for a film. These associations — which are themselves related — can be investigated by looking at ideas that had their most famous expression in the 1950s in France, and in the early 1960s in Britain. In France the advocates of the significance of mise-en-scène were the critics of the famous journal *Cahiers du Cinéma*, a number of whom (including François Truffaut, Jean-Luc Godard, Jacques Rivette, Eric

Rohmer and Claude Chabrol) subsequently became the film-makers of the *Nouvelle Vague*. In Britain, the journal *Movie* was where these ideas were most systematically explored, although this account will also look at passages from some of the other small British film journals of the early 1960s including *Oxford Opinion*, a student magazine for which three of the four founder-editors of *Movie* wrote whilst undergraduates.

This was not the first flowering of these debates, but it has become the most famous. The journal *Sequence* had in the late 1940s, expounded a number of critical ideas that were very similar to those developed by *Cahiers du Cinéma* and *Movie*. However, *Sequence* is not quite so interesting to this enquiry because the journal did not refer to 'mise-en-scène', tending instead to write about 'film poetry'. There is a section in the Appendix which points the reader in the direction of further reading on this area of criticism.

Mise-en-scène and film authorship

The concept of mise-en-scène is intimately concerned with arguments contending that the director, rather than the scriptwriter, should be considered the artist responsible for a film. This association relies on the fact that mise-en-scène encompasses the areas of decision making for which the director is responsible.

The relationship between mise-en-scène and direction is very clearly illustrated in a definition of the term offered by Robin Wood in an article from the beginning of his critical career. The article appeared amongst the pages of *Definition*, one of a number of small film journals of the early 1960s which, following the intervention of *Oxford Opinion*, were engaged in a furious battle about the significance of film style and the weight which it should properly be accorded in film criticism.[1] It is neither the first or the last word on the subject, but it is amongst the clearest and most articulate evocations of mise-en-scène. Wood writes:

> A director is about to make a film. He has before him a script, camera, lights, décor, actors. What he does with them is mise-en-

scène, and it is precisely here that the artistic significance of the film, if any, lies. The director's business is to get the actors (with their co-operation and advice) to move, speak, gesture, register expressions in a certain manner, with certain inflections, at a certain tempo: whether he uses the actors to fulfil precisely a preconceived vision (one thinks of Hitchcock) or releases their ability to express *themselves* and creates through them (one thinks of Renoir) is a matter for the individual genius. It is his business to place the actors significantly within the décor, so that the décor itself becomes an actor; with the advice and co-operation of the cameraman, to compose and frame the shots; regulate the tempo and rhythm of movement within the frame and of the movement of the camera; to determine the lighting of the scene. In all this the director's decision is final. All this is mise-en-scène.

And much more, for we have so far considered only one shot. The movement of the film from shot to shot, the relation of one shot to all the other shots already taken or not, which will make up the finished film, cutting, montage, all this is mise-en-scène. And still more. For mise-en-scène is not all these things considered as sepa-rate and detachable items: it is also what fuses all these into one organic unity, and consequently more, much more, than the sum of its parts. The tone and atmosphere of the film, visual metaphor, the establishment of relationships between characters, the relation of all parts to the whole: all this is mise-en-scène. It is this final consid-eration of the quality that fuses all the parts into a unity that led Astruc to define mise-en-scène as "a certain way of extending the élans of the soul in the movements of the body: a song, a rhythm, a dance". It is this that makes the film, as an art, so much closer to music than to literature. One can sum up by defining mise-en-scène, with Doniol-Valcroze, quite simply as "the organisation of time and space". (1960/61: 10)

A series of important points immediately arise, which touch on a number of areas which are central to this chapter:

1. Here, mise-en-scène is almost synonymous with direction.
2. It is, in Wood's view, the quality of the mise-en-scène that determines the artistic merits of the film.
3. The script, on the other hand, is only one creative element among many at the director's disposal.
4. The relationship *between* different elements is very important. The director's role is not only to co-ordinate the contributions of the different artists collaborating on a film, but to fuse the different elements into 'one organic unity'. The definition also demonstrates an interest in what was described in the last chapter as coherence across a work.[2]
5. Atypically for a definition of mise-en-scène, editing and elements of the soundtrack are included.
6. The passage illustrates the sharing of ideas from both sides of the channel. Doniol-Valcroze was one of the founder editors of *Cahiers du Cinéma*, and the director of *L'Eau à la Bouche* (1960). Astruc was an important figure in French film criticism. His article 'La Camera Stylo', makes an early comparison of the director with author: 'The film-maker/author writes with his camera as a writer writes with his pen. ... How can one possibly distinguish between the man who conceives the work and the man who writes it? Could one imagine a Faulkner novel written by someone other than Faulkner? And would *Citizen Kane* be satisfactory in any other form than that given to it by Orson Welles?' (1948: 22)

Wood's definition is characteristic of writing concerned with mise-en-scène in its refusal to regard the script as central to the film-making process. It is clear that for Wood, the script is only one of a number of elements at the director's disposal, only one ingredient that will contribute to the finished film. In articles in *Oxford Opinion* and *Movie*, V.F. Perkins quotes a remark by the director Nicholas Ray that makes this point rather well: '"It was all in the script" a disillusioned writer will tell you. But it was never all in the script. If it were, why make the movie?' (1956: 71).

Perkins develops Ray's remark, in the *Movie* article, arguing that:

> The disillusioned writer and the insensitive critic are alike in discounting the very thing for which one goes to the cinema: the extraordinary resonances which a director can provoke by his use of actors, decor, movement, colour, shape, of all that can be seen and heard. (1963b: 5)

This sense of the transformative affect of film style is extremely important. It is by means of the mise-en-scène that the director turns a script into a film.

Comparatively, Wood and Perkins are measured in their remarks: many of the writers of *Cahiers du Cinéma* have gone further than this in their celebration of direction over scriptwriting. Fereydoun Hoveyda's review of *Party Girl* (Nicholas Ray, 1958) makes a similar case more polemically:

> *Party Girl* has an idiotic story. So what? If the substratum of cinematic work was made up simply of plot convolutions unravelling on the screen, then we could just annex the Seventh Art to literature, be content with illustrating novels and short stories (which is precisely what happens with a great many films we do not admire), and hand over *Cahiers* to literary critics. ... *Party Girl* comes just at the right moment to remind us that what constitutes the essence of cinema is nothing other than *mise en scène*. It is *mise en scène* which gives expression to everything on the screen, transforming, as if by magic, a screenplay written by someone else into something which is truly an author's film. (1960a: 123)

An example of the transformative effect of mise-en-scène

If we take a momentary break from the historical discussion, we can reflect on the transformative power of mise-en-scène in some of the examples already encountered. In the example from *Notorious*, the meanings of the scene were not contained in the script, but in the treatment. In terms of plot and dialogue, the scene might be summarised as 'Devlin (Cary Grant) insinuates himself into one of Alicia's (Ingrid Bergman's) parties in order to get to know her'. Rather, it is the way in which the scene has been filmed that is significant: the lighting, the organisation of space, the blocking of the performers, the action of characters. It is the *realisation* that is important.

John Sayles wrote as well as directed and edited *Lone Star* and so one might imagine that the creative process was essentially one that happened at the writing stage. However, it is revealing that in the published screenplay many of the details which were important to the interpretation set out in Chapter 2 do not appear. The dialogue remains much the same, but in the screenplay Chucho draws the line with his heel rather than with the bottle of *CocaCola* (from which he is nevertheless drinking). Moreover, Sam 'obliges' when he is asked to step over the line, and later, smiling, 'plays with the line with his toe' (Sayles 1998: 194). Not only the tone but also the meanings of the scene have been established in production. As Sayles writes in the introduction to the screenplays (it is published together with the script of Sayles' subsequent film *Men With Guns*):

> Reading these [screenplays] without having reference to the movies made from them may be a little stark. The music is not here, the acting, the visceral power of the locations, no camera movement or lighting — all the things that make a movie a movie. So try to take them as the blueprints they are, outlines that helped people come together and make a story. (1998: x)

Mise-en-scène and the medium

As Hoveyda's remarks on *Party Girl* suggest, mise-en-scène is bound up with arguments about a criticism which is sensitive to the way film works as a medium, rather than regarding film merely an adjunct to the novel. Mise-en-scène is unique to the cinema, and it is the way in which cinema is uniquely expressive. Jim Hillier, who has edited two collections of criticism from *Cahiers du Cinéma*, has called this aspect the 'cinemato-graphic specificity' of mise-en-scène (1985: 10). In doing so he is making reference to another article by Hoveyda, called 'Les Taches du Soleil', in which the critic, reflecting on *Cahiers'* criticism, writes, 'when we say [in the journal] that the specificity of the cinematographic work lies in its technique and not in its content, in its mise-en-scène and not in the screenplay and the dialogue, we raise a storm of protest' (1960b: 138).

Perkins, Hoveyda, and Wood share the opinion that critics will not be able to understand films unless they are sensitive to mise-en-scène. More challengingly perhaps, all argue that the quality of a film is based in the mise-en-scène. As Wood writes, 'it is precisely here that the artistic signif-icance of the film, if any, lies' (1960/61: 10). Importantly, the critics of *Cahiers* and *Movie* are *basing* their critical judgements on the grounds of mise-en-scène. V.F. Perkins again, this time from the article on Nicholas Ray in *Oxford Opinion*:

> [Ray is], in English-speaking countries, the most under-rated of all contemporary directors. The reasons for this are obvious enough: the majority of his films have been assignments — of the seven-teen Ray films so far seen in England only three have been overtly serious in intention. Moreover they are melodramas whose impor-tance derives not from what their characters do and say, but from the way in which they do and say it, the way in which they move, talk and look at one another. Thus the quality of the films is not literary, since it owes little to the original script, but cinematic; it results from the subjection of a frequently banal narrative to an idiosyn-cratic *mise-en-scène*. (1960a: 31)

In this passage, Perkins is not only grounding his claims for the films' quality in the mise-en-scène, but also his estimation of the director. It does not matter that Ray has not originated the stories because the quality of the films is not literary, it does not matter if Ray did not write all of his scripts, because it is not the scripts that the sensitive critic is admiring. Mise-en-scène can form the basis of an argument about authorship because if one recognises the expressive value of the mise-en-scène then the director must logically be the artist responsible.

Some of the other consequences of basing critical judgements on film style also become clear from Perkins' argument, particularly the challenge to traditional reasons for not taking popular films seriously. The implications of style-based criticism are most markedly shown in relation to Hollywood films, both because it is a cinema where directors may be assigned to projects rather than originate them, and because it is a cinema which works with stories which are not evidently 'art'. Mise-en-scène, in short, enabled the critics of *Cahiers du Cinéma* and *Movie* to discuss areas of cinema which had previously been dismissed out of hand.

Considered in terms of their plots and dialogue, films such as *Psycho*, *Rio Bravo*, *River of No Return* and *Party Girl* may not impress. Whilst *The Seventh Seal* appears to be 'concerned with such fundamentals as the nature of faith and the mystery of death', these American films are tales about cowboys or gangsters.[3] However, if the critic is attuned to the mise-en-scène, very different conclusions will be reached. To quote Robin Wood:

> If we regard *Rio Bravo* as words on paper, as a plot and dialogue merely, we shall see little beyond a well-constructed cowboy yarn. Analyse the *film* and you discover a profound sense of complex moral values, you find yourself analysing a powerful, supremely balanced, objective empirical intelligence. (1960/61: 11)

This point about the popular cinema is very important. Even the idea of authorship was only really contentious in relation to directors working in the 'commercial' cinema. A conception of film as the director's art had considerable currency in earlier criticism, but only in relation to certain kinds of cinema. Before the advent of *Cahiers* or *Movie*, critics were perfectly prepared to regard Eisenstein or Bergman as artists, but it was a very different situation when it came to Hollywood directors. Mise-en-scène criticism challenged deeply entrenched cultural values.

If the attention to stylistic detail and the emphasis on the director were controversial, then that was nothing to the films that were admired by critics following these approaches. Attacking the traditional 'insistence on the cinema as solely an intellectual medium rather than as a visual and sensual one' (Shivas 1960a: 39), the *Oxford Opinion* critics, for example, addressed Fuller's *The Crimson Kimono*, Minnelli's *Home from the Hill* and Boetticher's *Comanche Station* with a seriousness reserved elsewhere for *The Seventh Seal* or *L'Avventura*. Hitchcock was described as a 'trage-dian' by Perkins on the strength of *Psycho* (1960b: 35), and Ian Cameron contributed a study of the major concerns of the films of Frank Tashlin.[4]

Impact

It is difficult to get a sense of the outrage that these ideas engendered. Charles Barr, later to be associated with *Movie* but then writing about film for *Granta*, has described his first encounter with *Oxford Opinion*:

> I remember going to a bookshop in Cambridge, probably in my second year or so, and picking up this magazine *Oxford Opinion* and glancing through it and thinking, 'Oh it's got some writing about films, I'd better buy this'. And then reading the first issue of *Oxford Opinion* with the writing on film, and being rather outraged by it, rather shocked. It was obviously powerful writing but it seemed so wrong. ... Here were a lot of films that I either hadn't heard of or just assumed were very minor, like a Randolph Scott B-western. It was exciting but it seemed deeply wrong, unsettling, rather outrageous.[5]

Famously, Penelope Houston, the longstanding editor of *Sight and Sound*, responded to the challenge of *Oxford Opinion* with the rebuttal, 'Cinema is about the human situation, not about "spatial relationships"' (1960: 163). The silliness of this maxim was noted by a number of writers at the time. Raymond Durgnat, in a witty and irreverent article for the journal *Motion*, pointed out that: 'The only formulation that begins to make sense is to say that the "spatial relationships" in Ray, Lang, Antonioni, Mizoguchi et al are the human relationships in metaphor' (1963: 39).[6]

Houston's remark is typical of *Sight and Sound*, and perhaps more widely of the orthodoxy of British film culture of this time, in its refusal to recognise the relationship between form and content, between style and meaning that the critics of *Cahiers* and *Movie* advocated. Her marked presumption is that an interest in 'spatial relationships' precludes an interest in 'subject'. Whereas the tenor of mise-en-scène-sensitive criticism is that style determines meaning, that 'How is What', that 'tracking shots', as Godard once provocatively remarked, 'are a question of morality' (Hillier 1985: 62).[7]

Editing and sound

Examining this history also helps us make sense of some of mise-en-scène's stranger characteristics. Wood's definition of mise-en-scène is unusual in that it includes editing, and sound (even if only in terms of the intonation that the cast give to the dialogue). It is more usual for mise-en-scène to refer exclusively to *visual* style, and not to cater for the range of decision-making involved in the creation of the soundtrack. The traditional deafness of mise-en-scène may be partly explained as part of the polemical desire to celebrate what is visual, what is non-literal, precisely those elements which are *not* the dialogue. But it may also relate to the fact that the commissioned director would not always have full control over the soundtrack.

There are notable cases where this is the case: Douglas Sirk's 1953 film *All I Desire* is a good example. In a fine article on the film in one of the more recent issues of *Movie*, Michael Walker points out that 'apart from one musical theme, the score is cobbled together from bits of previous scores. ... We hear not only the Liszt piano theme used in *Letter from an Unknown Woman* (1948), but, more disconcertingly, parts of Frank Skinner's score for *Black Angel* (1946) and parts of Miklos Rozsa's score for *Secret Beyond the Door* (1947) at various points in the movie' (1990: 32).

The exclusion of editing also relates to the polemical arguments which sought to find value in the work of Hollywood directors. In the worst case scenario, where the director does not have control over the cutting, the casting, the script or the soundtrack of a film, what she or he *does* control is the mise-en-scène. Thus Charles Barr, whilst discussing the way in which a number of Ray's films were re-cut by the studio, can argue:

> Of course it would be wonderful to see *The James Brothers* and *Bitter Victory* and *Wind Across the Everglades* in the form Ray intended ... but Ray's films, like Stroheim's, are weakened comparatively little, because of [his] control over texture. (1962a: 25)

It should be clear that in practice considering mise-en-scène without also thinking about sound and dialogue may prove rather limiting. So often it is the interaction between these different channels of communication that is stimulating. It may not even be possible, in some situations, to talk about elements of mise-en-scène without also referring to editing, as the discussion of the scene from *Lone Star* reveals. When discussing a long take, when does one stop talking about mise-en-scène and start talking about editing? After all, one of the most significant artistic decisions about a long take is when to bring it to an end. Nevertheless, if mise-en-scène had a polemical edge at this time, it was because it was so necessary to focus attention on the elements of which it is comprised. One of the most important functions of mise-en-scène as a critical concept remains the way in which it draws attention to, and makes easier to discuss, all of those elements which communicate non-verbally.

Conclusion

Mise-en-scène's particular association with Hollywood film has two bases, therefore. Firstly, through its historical role in opening up popular cinema to serious consideration. Secondly, because Hollywood films may *only* reveal their qualities if one is thinking about them in terms of mise-en-scène.

At the same time, one should not make the mistake of thinking that mise-en-scène is only relevant to popular cinema. Although the debate about Hollywood demonstrates what is at stake in mise-en-scène particularly clearly, these ideas are just as relevant to other forms of cinema. Nor should one assume, for that matter, that the critics of *Cahiers du Cinéma* and *Movie* were only interested in Hollywood films — both journals devoted as much space (and the same approaches) to European cinema as North American.

Ultimately, the concept of mise-en-scène may be more important than the arguments about authorship which it supported. It enabled critics to understand film as a visual and sensory experience rather than just a literary one, to engage with film as medium in its own right, and to consider the determining influence of style upon meaning. And, in the case of *Movie* particularly, it formed the basis of a detailed criticism, which strove to understand the relationship between a film's meanings and the evidence on the screen. Mise-en-scène criticism made possible a more profound sense of how films work.

5   MISE-EN-SCÈNE AND MELODRAMA

Melodrama has always proved rich in its visual style. Laura Mulvey has gone so far as to call melodrama 'the genre of mise-en-scène, site of emotions that cannot be expressed in so many words' (1996: 29). Certainly melodrama demonstrates par excellence the ability of Hollywood film and popular cinema more generally, to express things visually rather than verbally. This chapter examines criticism and other writing on Hollywood melodrama, in order to consider some of the ideas about mise-en-scène that appear in this context.

A very brief history

In every day usage, 'melodrama' is frequently used pejoratively. One of the exciting areas of recent criticism in a number of disciplines, however, has been a reappraisal of the traditions of melodrama. Peter Brooks' book *The Melodramatic Imagination: Balzac, Henry James, Melodrama, and the Mode of Excess* (1976), which has been seized upon with particular enthusiasm by film critics and theorists, explores the way in which melodrama is a pervasive, if often unrecognised, cultural form. Brooks traces melodrama's origins to the illegitimate theatre of pre-Revolutionary France — illegitimate because as a form of censorship, only the three official, 'patented' theatres were allowed to use dialogue.[1] In enforced silence, a tradition of richly visual expression developed. When the restrictions ended with the revolution, the form continued and expanded, consolidating into what Brooks describes as the 'classical' period between 1800 and 1830, and eventually becoming the dominant theatrical tradition of the nineteenth century, shaping the Romantic movement, and forming the major mode of expression in the novels of Charles Dickens, Charlotte Brontë and Henry James.

Hollywood film has a dual relationship to this tradition: firstly, a direct connection in terms of conventions and (popular) audience, which the silent cinema inherited from theatrical melodrama at the beginning of the twentieth century; secondly, an analogous relationship, in terms of silence in the medium's formative years (and subsequently, a silence of a different kind enforced through the means of the Motion Picture Production Code). In each case, the circumstances helped to foster other ways of expressing things which could not be directly stated, and provided a powerful impetus toward the visual dramatisation of themes.

At one level, large amounts of Hollywood cinema are melodramatic, not merely a single genre. Deborah Thomas, in her recent book *Beyond Genre* (2000), argues that the 'melodramatic' exists alongside the 'comedic' and the 'romantic', as a mode of expression which cuts across traditional generic boundaries. Michael Walker, in his comprehensive article 'Melodrama and the American Cinema' from 1982, also identifies a broad melodramatic tradition in Hollywood cinema, within which he identifies two categories: melodramas of action (which include westerns, crime thrillers, and adventure films) and melodramas of passion. Most frequently in modern film criticism, however, 'melodrama' is used to refer to what Walker calls the 'melodramas of passion': the woman's film; romantic melodramas; family and/or small-town melodramas; melodramas in the gothic tradition.

In critical terms as well, melodrama has a long association with mise-en-scène. T.S. Eliot, writing in 1927 about the melodramatic tradition and its relationship to the novels of Wilkie Collins and Charles Dickens, celebrates mise-en-scène in the work both authors.[2] Moreover, critical writing about film melodrama is rich in the ways critics have conceived of mise-en-scène, and these different conceptions are the subject of this chapter.

Décor and Character

Critics have often discussed the way that décor can express a character's emotions or predicament. In this, critics are not simply thinking about the way in which the design or furnishing of a character's home or bedroom may tell us something about that individual, although that can be of interest, but also the way in which the background or composition of a shot can express what a character may not be able to put into words.

This approach has a history which precedes the critical 'discovery' of film melodrama (which belatedly took place in the early 1970s). Cameron provides an example of this kind of interpretation in *Oxford Opinion*, praising *The Fugitive Kind* (1959), an adaptation of Tennessee Williams' play *Orpheus Descending*, directed by Sydney Lumet:

> Lumet uses settings to bring out the recurrence theme which seems to have interested him most. He has taken advantage of the freedom of setting which the play lacked to place Lady's description of her father's death in the ruins of his wine-garden. She leans against a charred wooden beam as she talks, and when she says 'I'm full of hate', the burned-out ruins become a potent image of her hate and barrenness. In the background we see the fresh young saplings which have pushed their way up through the ruins to foreshadow the change which is just starting to come over Lady. (1960e: 45)

There are a number of points in *Movie* where critics apply a similar approach, including an article by Barry Boys which looks at Minnelli's film *The Courtship of Eddie's Father* (1963). The recently bereaved father and son are preparing lunch (an activity with which they are unfamiliar) on the day that Eddie has returned to school after the death of his mother. Eddie mentions to his father that he wanted to cry at school, but did not.

> Eddie is standing on a stool getting crockery out of a cupboard. On the last line he is carefully putting a cup on its saucer. Balanced on

the stool, holding a breakable object suggests the fragility of his
emotional state, which is later shown in the hysterical reaction to a
dead fish in his bedroom. (1963: 29)

The Courtship of Eddie's Father is a romantic comedy, although this is
one of its more melodramatic scenes.[3] However, in early *Movie* criticism
mise-en-scène is discussed in relation to the director and not in relation
to genre. It is Thomas Elsaesser's groundbreaking article 'Tales of
Sound and Fury' from the journal *Monogram* which claims a particular
relationship between melodrama and mise-en-scène, and identifies
the expressive relationship of décor to character as characteristically
melodramatic. Elsaesser argues that 'the domestic melodrama in colour
and widescreen, as it appeared in the '40's and '50s [is] the most highly
elaborated, complex mode of cinematic signification that the American
Cinema has ever produced' (1972: 7). Both physical and psychical
characteristics of the genre, he argues, make it particularly amenable
to mise-en-scène:

FIGURE 32 *All That Heaven Allows*: The décor reflects Cary's (Jane Wyman) entrapment within the middle
class home

> The melodrama is iconographically fixed by the claustrophobic atmosphere of the bourgeois home and/or the small-town setting, its emotional pattern is that of panic and latent hysteria, reinforced stylistically by a complex handling of space in interiors (Sirk, Ray and Losey particularly excel in this) to the point where the world seems totally predetermined and pervaded by 'meaning' and interpretable signs. (Quoted in Gledhill 1987: 62)[4]

In other words, not only does the domestic setting provide an enormous range of plastic and spatial opportunities for film-makers to create suggestive mise-en-scène, but also, in contrast to what Elsaesser calls the 'action genres' — musicals or westerns, for instance — the characters of domestic melodramas have no outlet for their emotions.

In the action genres, such conflicts can be successfully 'externalised and projected into direct action', but in the melodrama the physical and social sphere in which the characters live means that they cannot openly express themselves or resolve concerns through dance or decisive action. As a result, Elsaesser argues, we witness 'a sublimation of dramatic conflict into decor, colour, gesture and composition of the frame, which in the best melodramas is perfectly thematised in terms of the characters' emotional and psychological predicaments' (1972: 7):

> When Minnelli's characters find themselves in an emotionally precarious or contradictory situation, it often affects the 'balance' of the visual composition — wine glasses, a piece of china or a trayful of drinks emphasise their situation. ... When Robert Stack in *Written on the Wind*, standing by the window he has just opened to get some fresh air into an extremely heavy family atmosphere, hears of Lauren Bacall expecting a baby, the most eloquent thing about his misery is the way in which he squeezes himself into the frame of the half-open window, every word his wife says to him bringing torment to his lacerated soul and racked body. (1972: 11)

Cinematic counterpoint

'Tales of Sound and Fury' is of particular importance to this chapter because it contains three or four different ways of conceptualising mise-en-scène. In a passage which appears in the original version of the article, but which has been excised from the edited version found in collections, Elsaesser advances a concept he calls 'cinematic counterpoint'. This idea, which is concerned with the kind of visual correspondences discussed in Chapter 3, examines the way in which 'structural parallels' can be used to undermine apparent moral contrasts. It offers a suggestive account of the way in which a film's style can work to qualify and complicate the apparent assertion of the narrative:

> If hero and villain, for instance, are seen doing trivial acts in a similar way (wash their hands, or eat a fried egg) the apparently non-significant (visual) parallel will help to modify the apparently all-important (moral) contrast. A parallelism on the level of overt intrigue or suspense (a repeated piece of action at a dramatically emphatic point — the hero and villain both slamming the door, or passing the same street corner in hot pursuit of the heroine) will on the other hand tend to reinforce the moral contrast. Griffith uses his cross-cutting in both these ways. This illustrates a principle one might call cinematic counterpoint: in the latter example, stylistic means, i.e. the lower register of punctuation (parallel montage, cross-cutting, visual repetition, musical accompaniment) serves to intensify the melodic line of the upper register (the story, the intrigue); in the former case, the same techniques are used to construct a different line 'against the current', which if developed consistently, can constitute itself as a theme in its own right.
>
> The difference is one of stylistics, of emphasis or 'soft-pedalling' in the telling of the tale. It is one of the ways American films have always been able to 'contradict' or subvert their manifest moral intent or ideological bias. This is particularly important when one discusses the melodrama with a happy ending, because the stylistic

countercurrent is often so strong that it makes the story and its resolution bristle with a kind of built-in resistance to its own facile optimism — if one cares to look closely. (1972: 6)

Mise-en-scène and point of view

'Tales of Sound and Fury' is also distinguished by an understanding of point of view, its relationship to mise-en-scène, and the specific qualities of point of view in melodrama. Elsaesser discusses the significance of the differing levels of awareness between audience and character in terms of irony and pathos. 'Pathos results from non-communication or silence made eloquent', he writes (1972: 14). Mentioning scenes such as the daughter's wedding in *Stella Dallas* (1937), or Naomi's (Barbara Stanwyck's) unnoticed return in *All I Desire* (1953), Elsaesser continues:

> Such archetypal melodramatic situations activate very strongly an audience's participation, for there is a desire to make up for the emotional deficiency, to impart the different awareness, which in other genres is systematically frustrated to produce suspense: the primitive desire to warn the heroine of the perils looming visibly over her in the shape of the villain's shadow. But in the more sophisticated melodramas this pathos is most acutely produced through a 'liberal' mise-en-scène which balances points of view, so that the spectator is in a position of seeing and evaluating contrasting attitudes within a given thematic framework — a framework which is the result of the total configuration and therefore inaccessible to the protagonists themselves. (1972: 15)

Often a film audience are 'privileged' over a character because they have access to information which the character does not. What is very interesting about Elsaesser's observations here is that they recognise that such a difference of awareness — and more complex balances of perspective — can result from the texture of the image rather than simply from the control of narrative information. Elsaesser also notes that this process

FIGURE 33 *There's Always Tomorrow*

may be harnessed to reveal 'how ideological contradictions are reflected in the character's seemingly spontaneous behaviour' (1972: 14).

An image from *There's Always Tomorrow* (Douglas Sirk, 1955) which exemplifies this process illustrates the article, although it is not discussed by Elsaesser. The still is from the conclusion of the sequence in which Marion Groves (Joan Bennett) has completely, and from the audience's point of view frustratingly, failed to recognise the feelings of entrapment and disillusionment which her husband Clifford (Fred MacMurray) is trying to express. Marion sits down at her dressing table, her reflection caught in the make-up mirror, and lists the domestic duties which she must undertake the following day. Thus, framing Marion within the frame, the mise-en-scène provides the spectator with a balancing perspective of which Marion herself is unaware: that she is as much a victim of the daily oppressions and repressions of her role in family life as her husband is in his.

This is precisely the kind of effect that Laura Mulvey also has in mind when discussing the mise-en-scène of melodrama in her article 'Notes on Sirk and Melodrama'. Mulvey too is very intrigued by the relationship between the limits of the understanding of the central characters and the way in which the films can encourage the audience to perceive the action. She writes:

> The implications and poignancy of a particular narrative cannot be evoked wholly by limited characters with restricted dramatic functions — they do not fully grasp the forces they are up against or their own instinctive behaviour. It is here that the formal devices of Hollywood melodrama, as analysed by Thomas Elsaesser (in *Monogram* 4), contribute a transcendent, wordless commentary, giving abstract emotion spectacular form, contributing a narrative level that provides the action with a specific coherence. Mise-en-scène, rather than undercutting the action and the words of the story level, provides a central point of orientation for the spectator. (1977/78: 55)

Distanciation

When Mulvey writes about the mise-en-scène working to undercut the narrative level of the film, she is in part referring to another way of thinking about visual style, particularly in melodrama, where critics have argued that the mise-en-scène can create a 'distanciation effect' similar to those advocated by Bertolt Brecht in his writing on theatre. The *verfremdungseffekt* (which used to be translated as 'alienation effect' but is now more usually referred to as 'distanciation') refers to those elements of Brechtian theatrical practice which, rather than involving the audience in the emotional experience of the characters, instead encourage the spectator to become aware of the social forces that shape their behaviour. As Brecht writes in 'The Street Scene':

> What is involved here is, briefly, a technique of taking the human social incidents to be portrayed and labelling them as something striking, something that calls for explanation, is not to be taken for granted, not just natural. The object of this 'effect' is to allow

the spectator to criticize constructively from a social point of view. (1964, 125).

Often, though not exclusively, such moments of distanciation will be reflexive. That is, the play (or film) will draw attention to its own construction, so that there is no danger of the spectator being drawn unthinkingly into the action. Instead, an actor might step out of character and talk to the audience directly, or the different elements of perform-ance will be separated and set one against another.

In *Movie* several writers had identified these kinds of tactics in a film's mise-en-scène. Mark Shivas, for example, argues that in *Landru* (Claude Chabrol, 1962) a degree of stylisation shapes the spectator's relationship with the film's ambivalent protagonist:

> Chabrol's colour and décor ... give a certain "distancing" effect to the story, which allows us to look at Landru as an ordinary man, but at the same time to look at him as a myth in action. Many of the sets have the three-sided look of a tiny stage. ... Landru's country cottage has a stairway leading steeply out of the centre of its down-stairs room, covered in a carpet of uneasy red. The courtroom, even, is in pastel colours; the railway station where Landru asks so often for one single and one return ticket seems solid enough, but there is at the same time a feeling of reconstruction, of the historical tableau about it. (1963: 7–8)

Whilst on the subject of definitions, it is worth pointing out the distinc-tion between distanciation and distance (which Shivas might be felt to conflate with his expression '"distancing" effect'). 'Distance' is also a way of describing the extent of our involvement with a character, without going quite so far as to call into question the standing of the fictional world. The term also has different roots, in this case the literary critical discussion of the nineteenth-century novel. Mise-en-scène criticism has been traditionally interested in 'distance' too, and the word appears in some of the passages quoted in earlier chapters. The writing which

Mulvey specifically refers to includes a pair of articles by Paul Willemen, 'Distanciation and Douglas Sirk' and 'Towards an Analysis of the Sirkian System', which appeared in the journal *Screen*. The articles explore Sirk's films in relation to the artistic movements with which the director was familiar in the early part of his career in 1920s and 1930s Germany — not only Brecht but also expressionism and symbolism. Willemen's articles had a useful role in drawing attention to distanciation in the debates around melodrama, and may have helped to open a discussion of the influence of European modernism on Hollywood film. (Sirk was by no means the only exile to be working in Hollywood — Ophuls, Lang, Renoir, Brecht and many others found themselves in Hollywood during the late 1930s or during the 1939—45 war. One of the reasons why the Hollywood of the 1940s and 1950s is so rich is this encounter between high modernism and the entertainment capital of the world (see Britton 1991/92: 38).) However, the articles are marred by a poor grasp of the detail of the films they attempt to discuss, and by their dismissive attitude to the genre and its audience (the tenor of 'Distanciation and Douglas Sirk' is to celebrate the way in which the European intellectual Sirk subverted the 'weepie'). Furthermore, the articles have great difficulty reconciling the undoubted emotional effect of the films with the different levels of irony and distance equally apparent.[5]

Distance and involvement

It appears that the models of mise-en-scène offered by Mulvey and Elsaesser engage much more successfully with the delicate balance between the intense involvement with characters and the critical distance which melodramas often offer to their audiences. Films such as *Letter from an Unknown Woman* (Max Ophuls, 1948), *Imitation of Life* or *All That Heaven Allows* (Douglas Sirk, 1954) can be extremely moving and, simultaneously, encourage us to look beyond the characters to understand the larger forces that shape their behaviour. Following in the footsteps of Elsaesser and Mulvey, Bruce Babington and Peter Evans argue that 'empathy and detachment exist in a mutually qualifying relationship', and term this balance 'critical pathos' — 'empathy qualified but not destroyed by critical understanding' (Babington & Evans 1990: 50).

A good example of how such a complex balance of perspectives can be achieved by mise-en-scène is identified by Robin Wood in *Personal Views*. Wood, who has been discussing the way in which *Letter from an Unknown Woman* is constructed on a series of echoes and repetitions, writes:

> Ophuls' fondness for 'echoes' is not restricted to the 'twinning' of scenes or incidents: it is expressed equally through the minutiae of the *mise-en-scène*, the positioning of the camera, its angles, its distance, its movements. Occasionally, Ophuls creates a delicate irony solely through the use of the camera: about to leave for Linz, Lisa runs from the station at the last moment, intending to offer herself to Stefan. Finding him out, she awaits him on the stairs just above the door to his apartment. (The location has already accumulated certain emotional associations: it is where Lisa earlier crept during the night to listen to Stefan playing the piano.) Stefan comes home, but with another woman. We watch their entrance into the hallway (accompanied by the already familiar exchange with the hall porter: 'Who is it?' etc.) almost from Lisa's position, the camera just behind her, looking down at them, panning left to right as they come up the stairs and disappear into the apartment. The effect is close to that of a subjective shot, encouraging us to share Lisa's disillusionment very directly: she leaves for Linz. Some years (though only about ten minutes of screen time) later, we have the sequence of Lisa's evening with Stefan: the visit to a café frequented by musicians, the gift of the white rose, the lobster dinner, the enchanted visit to the deserted, out-of-season Prada, the dance. Finally, Stefan takes her home with him: it is the ideal culmination and fulfilment of Lisa's romantic fantasy. Ophuls comments on it — and distances us again from Lisa's enchantment — by recapitulating the earlier shot's *mise-en-scène*: again we look down on the lovers from the stairs, again the camera pans to show them entering the apartment, and Lisa becomes but one woman in a never-ending succession — to

Stefan, the suggestion is scarcely distinguishable from the others, though the suggestion is qualified by other details in the preceding sequence. (1976: 128–9)

More recently, this same pair of moments from the film have been examined by George M. Wilson. His interpretation is very similar to Wood's, but continues:

> But there is more suggested than this. In the second shot, given its relation to the first, the visible absence of Lisa as observer of the scene makes salient that she is now merely the subject of *our* perception and is utterly removed from the perspective that earlier she had held. (If the first of these shots had been a subjective shot that directly presented her field of vision and thus excluded her wholly from the frame, then the echoing second shot would not mark as it does her earlier complicity and later lack of complicity with the camera's point of view.) This simple strategy of echoing with a variation yields the sense, almost as an overtone to the second shot, that Lisa at this juncture lacks any consciousness of herself as an element in a mere recurrence of an event that had overwhelmed her consciousness. (1986: 103–4)

The pair of shots are a splendid example of extremely complex perspectives on the action articulated and balanced by the choice of where to place actors and camera. They also exemplify the balance of empathy and distance that characterises the great melodramas. We too have been touched by the evening, we are engaged with Lisa's aspirations, but we are not allowed by the film to lose sight of the perception that Lisa is driven by a romantic fantasy. Moments like this give substance to the idea that the great Hollywood melodramas offer 'a form of American Epic theatre which is frequently very much more complex and profound than the plays of Brecht himself' (Britton 1991/2: 38).

Letter from an Unknown Woman is one of the great works of the cinema and it has also been the subject of some outstanding criticism.

FIGURE 34 *Letter From an Unknown Woman*: Lisa (Joan Fontaine) watches Stefan (Louis Jourdan) return to his apartment with another woman

FIGURE 35

FIGURE 36 Lisa and Stefan return to the apartment

FIGURE 37

If one is interested in exploring ideas of distance and empathy, and other aspects of skilful style-based criticism, then there are not many places better to turn to than the writing on this film. (See the Appendix for more details.)

Point of view

Not for the first time in this book, discussion of mise-en-scène has lead rapidly into a complex discussion of point of view. In Chapter 1 the discussion of camera position and camera movement was concerned with the ways in which they shape the audience's relationship to action and characters. The discussion of visual 'linkages' between different parts of a film in Chapter 3 indicated ways in which the audience were given perspectives which were not available to the characters. All of the ways of understanding melodramatic mise-en-scène discussed in this chapter have been concerned with point of view, some of them very directly. The discussion in Chapter 6 heads in this direction again.

I shall not attempt to explore point of view here, despite the fact that it is such an important concept to any attempt to articulate the complexity of our response to film. Rather, I want to draw attention to how intimately mise-en-scène and point of view are connected, and then indicate where one can find a proper discussion. Douglas Pye's article 'Movies and Point of View', which was referred to in Chapter 1, is the best place to start. The article distinguishes very helpfully between different 'axes' of point of view. These axes include the 'spatial', which concerns the ways we are physically placed in relation to the action by the camera; the 'cognitive', which refers to the rate of flow of narrative information to characters and to the audience; and the 'evaluative', which is a way of talking about the kinds of judgements we make about characters and their actions whilst watching a film. The article develops its discussion through detailed analyses of sequences from *The Lusty Men* and *Rio Bravo*. George M. Wilson's *Narration in Light*, a passage of which we have just been examining, is sub-titled 'Studies in Cinematic Point of View' and is another of the best pieces of writing on the subject.

6   CASE STUDY: IMITATION OF LIFE

This chapter investigates an example which demonstrates in concrete terms a number of the features of the discussion of earlier chapters. *Imitation of Life* is a domestic melodrama, displaying the richness of visual style characteristic of the genre. It is a popular American film, very popular in fact — it was Universal's highest-ever grossing film until *Jaws* (Steven Spielberg, 1975). It was directed by Douglas Sirk, the cinematographer was Russell Metty, who worked with Sirk on a number of films and on other important Universal pictures of the period such as *Touch of Evil*.

This analysis focuses on a particular sequence, but as with previous examples it is not possible to talk about one sequence alone, and the discussion takes in stylistic strategies from across the film. A concluding section draws attention to the relationship of the analysis to approaches encountered earlier in the book.

The sequence we shall concentrate on takes place shortly after Annie (Juanita Moore) has been rejected by her daughter Sarah Jane (Susan Kohner) in Los Angeles. Susie (Sandra Dee) has stayed at home to look after Annie whilst her mother Lora (Lana Turner) and Steve (John Gavin) have gone to the screening of Lora's Italian film, and the ensuing party. From the moment when the scene begins until the moment Susie looks out of the window, the sequence consists of five shots: an establishing shot, two close ups of Annie and two close ups of Susie.

The bedside sequence

When the scene commences, Susie is in full flow, relaying her version of events earlier in the evening to Annie. As the scene progresses Susie proceeds to unburden thoughts of her love for Steve, whilst Annie's responses delicately attempt to steer Susie toward the reality of her situation.

Susie … and I know mother didn't understand. Oh, it was *so* embarrassing. And poor Steve, I mean what could he do? She just swept over him like a tidal wave.

Annie Now honey, it's only natural he'd like to go out with your mother, he always enjoyed her company. You remember that.

Susie But it's different now. All summer long it's been Steve and me. (*pause*) Annie, you know don't you.

Annie Know what?

Susie That I'm in love with Steve. I've always been in love with Steve, and always will be.

Annie Sure Susie, but like a little girl.

Susie No, I don't think it even started like that. In a funny way I always knew. Every time I thought I liked a boy it was because he reminded me of Steve, and then I'd stop liking him because … because he wasn't Steve.

The sequence begins with an establishing shot which is bisected vertically by a bedpost at the head of Annie's bed. To the left of this divide we can see Annie propped up by a pillow, her bed running toward the camera and the left hand side of the frame. To the right, in the foreground of the shot and facing the camera (although she turns around from time to time), sits Susie eating supper from a tray.

The right half of the image is colourful and cluttered. Susie is wearing a mauve jump-suit, a green lampshade extrudes from the upper right corner of the frame; in the distance is a bedside lamp. The table and tray are interposed between Susie and the camera, the chair at which she sits breaks

FIGURE 38 *Imitation of Life*: The establishing shot

up the space, the folds and pattern of the curtains form a backdrop. In contrast, the left half of the frame is bare and austere. The whites of the bed linen and the dark brown of the headboard, repeated in the wall and the shadow that falls across it above, are the predominant colours.

Annie, clearly unwell, lies very still, whereas Susie eats and chatters and gesticulates.

The comparative triviality of Susie's problems in relation to those suffered by Annie, apparent to the spectator from the narrative situation, is further evoked by the striking decisions of presentation. The fussiness of the right half of the frame contrasts with the bleakness of the left. The 'busy' decor associated with Susie is evocative of her privileged adolescence as witnessed earlier in the film. Her appearance and her surroundings are entirely in keeping with her world of picnics, yellow sweaters, thoroughbreds, imagined kissing and boys. Annie, on the other hand, is mourning for her lost daughter and the stark setting suggests something of the magnitude of the emotion involved. Indeed, this is Annie's death bed and Annie is increasingly removed from material considerations. It is to Annie's immense credit that she has time for Susie.

The choices concerning décor and camera position make available to the audience an insight into the relationships between the characters in the house. The schism of the establishing shot conveys a tremendous sense of two adjacent but virtually incompatible worlds, two lives lived contiguous to one another, but in different milieux. The choice of a wide angle lens exaggerates the distance between the actors, and further enforces our sense of the boundary between the two. (At one moment Susie takes a glass of milk from Annie, which is rather startling, because the lens had suggested such a substantial space between them.)

The position of the characters in relation to each other and the camera is significant in another respect. Two-shots where the audience can see both characters but one character has her or his back to the other are the stock-in-trade of melodrama, and the range of inflection that can be achieved through this simple arrangement is extremely variable. The most immediate consequence of such a framing is that the audience can read both characters' faces and so know more than either about how each is feeling. In this way the audience are privileged over the characters, and forms of dramatic irony can be rapidly established.

In this instance, the organisation of the visual field gives the spectator a more informed understanding of the scene than is available to Susie, both as a result of the blocking and the distinctions in décor. Not only can we see Annie and Susie all of the time, but also the division of the space which I have been describing can only be perceived by the audience. Indeed, viewed from another angle, the significance attributable to the décor would be lost (or changed).

The ideas introduced by the establishing shot are consolidated and developed in the images that follow. The other set-ups used in the early part of the scene — a close-up of Annie in bed along a similar axis, a slightly wider shot of Susie at ninety degrees — rigorously maintain the distinction in décor and colour present in the long-shot. Neither does the separation afforded by individual shots collapse our sense of the dislocation between the characters. Moreover, the close-ups of Annie enable us

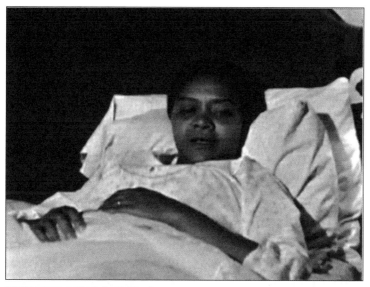

FIGURE 39 Close up of Annie (Juanita Moore)

FIGURE 40 Susie (Sandra Dee)

to perceive that which Susie does not notice. The first cut happens on the line 'Annie, you know don't you', but we are offered a close up of Annie which shows the degree of her suffering, rather than one of Susie, which would have served to make her declaration more emphatic.

Susie chatters on, paying little regard to Annie's remarks and, more importantly, oblivious to Annie's own situation. On the line, 'Sure Susie, but like a little girl', Annie turns away in obvious discomfort (there is an audible tightening of the breath) but Susie, looking away from Annie, fails to notice. Susie is so engrossed in her own conversation that she does not perceive that Annie has fallen asleep (or passed out?) for several moments. Returning from her reflection, Susie ascertains that Annie is asleep and turns out the light. She is about to leave the room when she hears the car pull up outside. She smiles indulgently as we watch her watching Lora and Steve through the window until, that is, she is dismayed to see them passionately embrace.

The pretensions of Susie's behaviour are clear to the audience: partly through our truer sense of the state of affairs between Lora, Steve and her; partly by the reversal of usual mother and daughter roles in this watching of the date returned home safely, and partly by the music which helps to cast the end of the scene in an ironic mode. The perception that Susie is *performing* the role of mother is one that is applicable to her behaviour throughout the sequence, however, and the way in which Sandra Dee performs Susie's romantic reflection and declamation enhances a suggestion of adolescent role play. She is trying out the role of the grown-up — and in doing so joins a whole cast of performers in the film.

Performance

Performance is the central motif of *Imitation of Life*. All of the main characters perform — Lora and Sarah Jane in particular, although Susie and Annie also have their moments. A major change that Sirk made to the initial outline given to him by producer Ross Hunter (and thereby to the novel by Fannie Hurst and the earlier film version of the story, directed by John Stahl) was to make Lora an actress (see Halliday 1997: 148; Mulvey 1996: 34). Yet,

759.13

city college

mise en scene
blade runner

3 weeks

Edward hopper biography.

as Richard Dyer has pointed out, we never see her on stage except in audition or receiving a curtain call (1977/78: 49). The logic of these decisions is that they provide the opportunity for examining Lora and the other characters engaging in the 'performance' of social roles.

As Dyer observes, 'Lora/Turner acts, puts on a performance, throughout the film'. Laura Mulvey writes that Lora is 'artificial to the point of self-reflexivity' (1996: 36). Consider the moment, discussed by Dyer, when Lora announces that, if necessary, she will give up Steve for the sake of her relationship with her daughter. As she delivers her lines, Lana Turner straightens, looks away from Susie, and sets her gaze toward the middle distance behind the camera (as if to the tenth row of the stalls). Susie's retort, 'Oh Mama, stop acting!', can be quite startling for the spectator, and Lora/Lana appears to be even more taken aback — the look of surprise in her eyes as she sharply turns her head is telling.

Lora's performance in life, as both Dyer and Mulvey have pointed out, is heavily dependent on Annie's backstage labours (Dyer 1977/8: 52; Mulvey

FIGURE 41 'Oh Mama, stop acting!'

1986: 33). Whilst Lora is walking to every agent on Broadway, Annie takes care of Susie, cleans and cooks, and addresses the letters with which Lora pays the bills. When Lora is on stage, Annie is keeping the home fires burning. Annie is often placed backstage — literally, in Lora's dressing room, and metaphorically in Lora's kitchen.

Additionally, in several scenes in the early part of the film, as Laura Mulvey has noted, Annie performs the role of maid in order to sustain Lora's own performance — most strikingly when Lora is attempting to persuade the agent Allen Loomis (Robert Alda) that she is an established Hollywood star. 'As the story develops, Annie's performance congeals into reality. ... While at first her "per-formance" invisibly supported Lora's visibility, her labour continues to support the household, materially and emotionally' (Mulvey 1996: 33). Sarah Jane is also literally a performer, but in a much less reputable sphere than the one in which Lora moves. It is Sarah Jane who is the clearest example of a character playing a social role: 'passing' as white is itself a form of performance. In the terrible scene of parting which is the prelude to Annie's incapacitation, Sarah Jane pretends to a friend that her mother is the nanny who brought her up. Annie, awfully, accepts this role. Is this the final irony, the blow which breaks Annie's heart: that after trying to dissuade Sarah Jane from passing, her love makes her take this part? Certainly, a hitherto unachieved indignity befalls Annie when she herself has to perform in order to sustain her daughter's deception, an agonising reprise of her earlier role for Lora.

On set and behind the scenes

The sense of the white and black characters living in proximate worlds separated by very real boundaries — as noted in relation to the bedside sequence — is another of the film's most important patterns. Even on the occasion of the first night in the cold-water flat, Sarah Jane complains that she and Annie 'always have to live in the back'. However, it is in Lora's grand house that the film begins to really work in this axis: in the difference between the kitchen, which is associated with Annie and Sarah Jane, and the palatial living area, associated with Lora and her public.

One of the most distinguished features of *Imitation of Life* is the way it marries this use of décor with the performance motif. A number of critics have noted how the house is itself rather like a stage set. More precisely, the way the décor is presented, and the ways in which the characters move within it, suggests the difference between the stage and the wings (or between on set and behind the camera). Annie is frequently to be found in the kitchen, preparing food for the guests, while Lora interacts in the vast living room. A crucial moment in this pattern, which illustrates both performance and spatial play, is the occasion when Sarah Jane serves Lora and guests with the tray of 'crawdaddies' carried above her head and a parody of 'coloured' behaviour.

Or consider the first night party for *No Greater Glory* which is held at the house. Steve, after a gap of many years, has just been reintroduced to Annie, Susie and Sarah Jane. This encounter takes place in the kitchen. Allen Loomis, now Lora's agent, summons Lora to rejoin her guests in the public part of the house: 'Well, are we holding the party in here?' Lora leads Susie and Steve out of the kitchen, arm in arm. Sarah Jane, having made to follow, stops abruptly. A reverse field cut shows us the three white characters disappearing together, presenting the image (if not the reality) of a nuclear family, before we cut again to look at Sarah Jane left in the kitchen. It is not a point of view figure, but it gives us a clear sense of her perspective nonetheless.[1]

The untold story

There are a number of moments in the film like this, where the camera goes out of its way to reveal Sarah Jane's, or more frequently Annie's, experience of scenes which are ostensibly about Lora or Susie. Another example would be the mute cut to Annie whilst Lora and David Edwards (Dan O'Herlihy) discuss the controversial 'coloured angle' of *No Greater Glory* making, as Dyer points out, no acknowledgement of Annie and waiting for her to serve them drinks.

In a scene parallel to the bedside sequence — this time involving Lora talking to Annie, one of the bedposts again dividing the image in half —

Annie reveals that Susie is in love with Steve. Lora rushes out of the room oblivious to Annie's plaintive 'Wait, Wait!' Annie sits up in bed as she says this, the only time in the scene when she lifts herself from the pillow, and the camera tracks in toward her. Sirk cuts whilst the camera movement is barely completed, which has the effect of drawing further attention to the disregard implied by, and involved in, the sudden exit.[2]

Annie's experiences happen behind the scenes and even off-camera. Certain moments in the film make it clear that Annie has a vibrant off-screen life. The funeral is the most emphatic, if retrospective, moment in this pattern. Lora's astonished and astonishing surprise that Annie should have a wealth of friends is another example, and one which illustrates the severe limits to Lora's understanding of Annie's experience.

Structural film-making

As film-maker, and champion of Sirk's films, Rainer Werner Fassbinder has observed, '*Imitation of Life* starts as a film about the Lana Turner character and turns quite imperceptibly into a film about Annie' (1972: 106). The film is constructed as a slow cross-fade from being more obviously a story about Lora and the hardships of her pursuit of stardom, to a story about the trials of Annie and Sarah Jane. At the same time, the two stories interlock — and the movement between the two sets of mothers and daughters is complex and crucial. *Imitation of Life* is not just a story about passing, and not just a story about a single mother's rise to stardom against adversity but rather it is both and, importantly, it is about the relationship between the two.

The film provides a central metaphor for this relationship in the stairways and landings that cross and re-cross Lora's home. The stairways are a physical representation of the two stories. There are the back stairs which lead diagonally up from the kitchen. Sarah Jane passes more freely through the house than her mother, but this is the stairway with which she is most clearly associated, using it to make her way to and from her secret rendezvous with her boyfriend. Then there is the route from the front door, the stairs that Lora uses, connected to the walkways that run above the public space of the front rooms. The most significant point, however, is the

FIGURE 42 The parallel scene

FIGURE 43 'Wait, Wait!'

junction where staircases and stories intersect. It is on this crossroads that Lora quizzes Sarah Jane about her date, the banisters placing Sarah Jane as if in a witness box, or even the dock. It is through the junction that Susie runs as she hurries back from Annie's bedroom to her own, on discovering Lora and Steve's relationship. It is here that Sarah Jane collapses after being attacked, and is attended to by both families.

The set helps the film solve its structural problem. In the design of Lora's house, Sirk has found a form for balancing the stories of both families. The very architecture of the house illustrates the way in which these characters' lives are interlinked but inequitably so.

Conclusion

By way of conclusion I want to underline the relationship between the analysis in this chapter and the ideas around mise-en-scène that we have encountered in Chapters 4 and 5.

We have examined the décor as being indicative of the characters' predicaments and emotions. A wealth of decisions about décor and framing in the bedside sequence, and in the rest of the film, can be understood in these terms. *Imitation of Life* also provides good examples of the stylistic excess of melodrama being inflected in order to create distanciation. We have already touched on the reflexive elements around Lora's performance, and we might extend this kind of observation to the décor, particularly the play between on-stage/set and off. A further example of this strategy is provided by the moment where Annie sets off to pack for her journey to Los Angeles. The camera tracks with her past an upright as she leaves the part of the room in which Lora and Steve are sitting, and when we look back with her, not only is the demarcation of space very apparent, but Lora and Steve are framed within a frame, almost suggesting that they are left in the world of the film while Annie has stepped out to reality.

If in these moments, however, the mise-en-scène performs a role rather like a distanciation effect, this is not to say that we lose sight of our emotional relationship to the characters. (In this particular example the moment may even increase our involvement with Annie, if not with Lora).

FIGURE 44 Annie steps out to reality

In the bedside scene, Susie's soliloquy is being delicately undermined but this does not entirely preclude the audience's sympathy for her. Rather, the mise-en-scène reminds us that there are questions of priority and perspective — and this scene offers us a perspective that she seems unable to adopt. In this sense the choices made in the realisation of the bedroom sequence furnish us with a very good example of mise-en-scène 'offering a wordless commentary on the action' and 'creating a central point of orientation for the spectator' (Mulvey 1977/78: 55). The sequence could also be accurately described, by Elsaesser, as possessing ...

> ... a 'liberal' mise-en-scène which balances points of view, so that the spectator is in a position of seeing and evaluating contrasting attitudes within a given thematic framework — a framework which is the result of the total configuration and therefore inaccessible to the protagonists themselves. (1972: 15)

That the perspectives we have considered are available to us and not the characters (at least not Susie) also returns us to the question of defining mise-en-scène, and the discussion at the end of Chapter 3. In the bedside sequence the camera's position is decisive in producing the perspective on the action: it is not possible to talk meaningfully about the mise-en-scène without (implicitly) referring to framing and composition.

Finally, being alive to the importance of the design of *Imitation of Life* is crucial: so much of the interrelationship between the two pairs of mothers and daughters is expressed visually. Without thinking about the film's structural analysis of the situation, one would miss the interaction of the two stories, and it is the interaction that gives the film complexity and its analysis strength. Without engaging with mise-en-scène, one would be hard pressed to perceive and discuss the meanings of a film in which the significant elements are not spoken but shown and felt. Looking back to the history discussed in Chapter 4, we might well reflect on the appropriateness of the idea that 'human relationships can be expressed in spatial terms' (Cameron, Perkins & Shivas 1960: 561).

CONCLUSION

It is appropriate to begin this conclusion by reflecting on a further distinction between the ways in which writers encountered in earlier chapters have conceptualised mise-en-scène. For the critics of *Cahiers du Cinéma*, *Movie*, and related publications, mise-en-scène was unambiguously concerned with the activities of the director. Indeed, I suggested in Chapter 4 that 'mise-en-scène' is almost synonymous with 'direction' in the definition provided by Robin Wood. Although mise-en-scène had a range of different implications for the criticism of this period, there was no question but that the director was responsible.

In Chapter 5 we examined some of the ways that mise-en-scène has been associated with a particular genre, or mode of expression. Thomas Elsaesser's 'Tales of Sound and Fury' has a foot in both camps in that it argues that domestic melodrama has particularly rich mise-en-scène, but the article also wants to identify the films directed by certain individuals as superior to the run of the mill. The article frequently refers to 'the best melodramas' or distinguishes the films of Nicholas Ray, Douglas Sirk and Vincente Minnelli from those directed by others. There is not necessarily a contradiction here — and on the evidence of the number of writers quoted who have celebrated the mise-en-scène of films from these directors, it does indeed seem that their work is particularly well achieved in these terms.

In writing from the years following the publication of 'Tales of Sound and Fury', the link between mise-en-scène and the director is often less secure. A number of theoretical movements have not wished to discuss films in relation to the director, yet sometimes still have wanted to talk about visual style. Here lies one of the useful aspects of the concept of mise-en-scène: it can be defined in relation to the director, but it does not have to be.

To put it another way, it is important to have a concept which helps us to focus on the objective features of the images on the screen. To be able to relate our sense of the meanings of a film back to the movement of the camera, a use of colour, or the organisation of décor and character is one of the reasons why a mise-en-scène approach makes for a most satisfying criticism to write and read. One of the great pleasures and advantages of a mise-en-scène, or a more generally style-based, approach is that it enables you to anchor your understanding of a film, and to support your arguments with evidence. It gives us a way of sharing and communicating enthusiasm for a film, and for making an interpretation persuasive. One of the things I have always responded to in the work of the writers featured here, is that their more abstract ideas and understanding are so clearly related to the concrete detail of the films under discussion.

There are also other features which make this tradition of writing stimulating. Mise-en-scène criticism is accessible, and does not depend on knowledge of an arcane set of terminology. It invites the reader to assess the validity of an argument against experience or against further viewing. Because mise-en-scène is so central to an understanding of how films work, it is also extremely relevant to the person reading film criticism in order to make films her/himself: attending to the relationship between style and meaning is a very good way of becoming aware of the consequences of your own stylistic decisions.

One of the most curious features of the history of Film Studies, given mise-en-scène's importance in establishing a mature standing for the subject, is that the concept subsequently became unpopular. This may have been partly because of mise-en-scène's association with arguments around authorship, at a time when the relationship between author and artwork was challenged on a number of fronts. It may be partly because of the arrival in the field of various forms of film theory, which tended to favour general arguments at the expense of the particular. And it may be partly, as I have argued elsewhere, that critical movements often denigrate that which precedes them in order to draw attention to their own novelty.[1] Whatever the causes, the result was that film style and its consequences became neglected in some quarters. Although it is the sort of thing that should never become unfashionable, mise-en-scène went out of fashion.

The advent of film theory helped to place a number of vital concerns and perspectives at the centre of academic enquiry. The social and political meanings of films became the focus of attention as never before. Nevertheless, I believe that the original arguments about film style continued to be as relevant as they ever were. If we are to be aware of the impact or import of a film, whatever theoretical or political frameworks we bring to bear, a true understanding of how that film works is essential. A number of critics before me have argued a similar case. For instance, Janey Place and Julianne Burton, writing in *Movie* in 1976, reason that:

> [C]ritics who confine themselves to chronicling changes in narrative content throughout the history of the cinema, ignoring the fact that the mediation of form is the final arbiter of a particular film's effect on the viewer, can never achieve more than an incomplete understanding of specific films and of the medium itself. (1976: 59)

A similar concern to bring together political enquiry with a precise and accurate criticism is also clear in the ambitions of the journal *CineAction!* (see Wood 1986; Jacobowitz 1986).

Other lessons which can usefully be taken from the historical arguments around mise-en-scène in Chapter 4, are not to judge a film by its ostensible subject and, especially, not to judge a film on pre-conceived notions of the conditions of its production. But today, one does not have to look further than the newspaper to discover the most extraordinary misapprehensions of what a popular film can or might be. The critical myopia and cultural snobbery which *Oxford Opinion* challenged when they attacked 'the implicitly accepted distinction between art and commerce' (Cameron 1960a: 36), where 'commerce tends to hail from west of Pinewood, especially from California; art, barring Cinecittà, from points east' (Shivas 1960a: 38–9), still exert an influence on today's cultural attitudes.

If any of the main points of this book are true — that style determines meaning, that how an event is portrayed on the screen defines its significance, that single moments or images of films cannot be adequately considered when extracted from their context — then close study continues to be vital. My belief is that an understanding of mise-en-scène is a prerequisite for making other kinds of claims about film, and, whatever argument you want to make, whatever the motivation for your discussion, a sense of how style relates to meaning needs to be central to your enquiry. As Gavin Lambert observed, in the last line of his article 'A Last Look Round', in the final issue of *Sequence*, 'Until we know how a film is speaking to us, we cannot be sure what it is saying' (1952: 7).

APPENDIX

As mentioned in the Introduction, one of the main aims of this book is to point the reader in the direction of the best writing on mise-en-scène. In addition to the articles discussed and quoted earlier, this appendix indicates where to find illuminating writing about films as film. A distinct bibliography of work cited in the text — which is the place to identify the sources indicated by references — appears at the back of the book.

Essential

Perkins, V.F. (1981) 'Moments of Choice', *The Movie*, Ch. 58, 1141–5. (Reprinted in A. Lloyd (ed.) (1982) *Movies of the Fifties*. London: Orbis Publishing, 209–13.)

This article is an excellent place to start. It contains a series of suggestive examples of the way in which different elements of mise-en-scène can be deployed expressively, although the term itself is not used. Instead, the article's approach is in terms of the director's decisions: Perkins discusses the opportunities within the image for making significant choices.

Perkins, V.F. (1972) *Film as Film: Understanding and Judging Movies*. Harmondsworth: Penguin.

Film as Film is the sort of book which you read as a newcomer to film but which you keep returning to. As was the case with 'Moments of Choice', Perkins avoids referring to 'mise-en-scène', but this study is full of interpretation of expressive visual style. It is also an excellent book from the point of view of its commitment to ideas of coherence and integration. Chapters 5, 'The World and its Image', and 6, 'How is What', are particularly recommended.

Wood, R. (1976) *Personal Views*. London: Gordon Fraser.

Alongside *Hitchcock's Films* (see below), this is one of Wood's books which is most concerned with mise-en-scène and the significance of film style. It includes sustained analyses of such films as *Touch of Evil* (Orson Welles, 1958), *The Scarlet Empress* (Josef von Sternberg, 1934), *The Reckless Moment* (Max Ophuls, 1949), *Meet Me in St Louis* (Vincent Minnelli, 1946), *I Walked With a Zombie* (Jacques Tourneur, 1943), and *Ugetsu Monogatari* (Kenji Mizoguchi, 1953).

Movie

The journal *Movie* continues to appear (but neither regularly nor frequently). A distinction can be made between the first 19 issues which we might call 'early *Movie*', and number 20 onwards (which appear in a different format). *Movie Reader*, a collection of articles from issues 1–19, was published in 1972. There is some really wonderful writing in the journal, both in the early years and in the more recent issues, which apply the same principles with greater depth and precision. In the 1970s some new writers joined the roster of contributors, including Andrew Britton whose work deftly combines a style-based approach with political analysis and a detailed knowledge of broader traditions of American art and culture. Current members of the editorial board, in addition to Ian Cameron and V.F. Perkins, include Deborah Thomas, Douglas Pye, Michael Walker, Charles Barr, Jim Hillier, Ed Gallafent, and Robin Wood.

In addition to articles featured in earlier chapters, some highlights from issues 1–19 include:

Cameron, I. (1962a) 'Films, Directors and Critics', *Movie*, 2, 4–7.

—— (ed.) (1972) *Movie Reader*. London: November Books.

Mayersberg, P. (1963) 'The Trial of Joan of Arc', *Movie*, 7, 30–2.

Perkins, V.F. (1962a) (on behalf of the editorial board) 'The British Cinema', *Movie*, 1, 2–7.

—— (1962b) 'River of no Return', *Movie*, 2, 18–19.

—— (1963) 'Rope', *Movie*, 7, 11–13.

From issue 20 onwards:

Britton, A. (1976) 'Mandingo', *Movie*, 22, 1–22.

Perkins, V.F. (1990b) 'Must We Say What They Mean?: Film Criticism and Interpretation', Movie, 34/35, 1–6.

Pye, D. (1975) 'Junior Bonner', *Movie*, 21, 22–5.

Thomas, D. (1990) 'Blonde Venus', *Movie*, 34/35, 7–15.

Wood, R. (1975) 'Smart-ass & Cutie-pie: Notes toward and evaluation of Altman' *Movie*, 21, 1–17.

Movie Books

The return of the '*Movie* books' has been an exciting development in film criticism over the last decade. *The Movie Book of Film Noir* (1992) and *The Movie Book of the Western* (1996) are exceptionally interesting collections of writing. Attention should also be drawn to other titles in this handsomely produced series: Andrew Britton's *Katharine Hepburn*, Deborah Thomas' *Beyond Genre*, Ed Gallafent's *Astaire & Rogers*, Charles Barr's *English Hitchcock*. Watch out, also, for the forthcoming edited collections *Unexplored Hitchcock* and *Fritz Lang*. These books are published by Ian Cameron, original editor of *Movie* (and editor of the film section of *Oxford Opinion*), under the imprint Cameron and Hollis. Fuller details below:

Barr, C. (1999) *English Hitchcock*. Moffat: Cameron & Hollis.

Britton, A. (1995) *Katharine Hepburn: Star as Feminist*. London: Studio Vista.

Cameron, I. (ed.) (1992) *The Movie Book of Film Noir.* London: Studio Vista.

Cameron, I. and D. Pye (eds) (1996) *The Movie Book of the Western.* London: Studio Vista.

Gallafent, E. (2000) *Astaire & Rogers.* Moffat: Cameron & Hollis.

CineAction!

The other journal that is a good place to look for detailed, style-sensitive criticism is *CineAction!* This is edited on a rotational basis and the different interests of the members of the editorial collective are reflected in particular issues. From the beginning, however, one of the journal's stated ambitions has been to combine a detailed approach with political criticism.

Articles of particular interest include:

Britton, A. (1991/92) 'A New Servitude: Bette Davis, Now Voyager and the Radicalism of the Woman's Film', *CineAction!*, 26/27, 32–59.

___ (1993) 'Meet Me in St Louis: Smith, or the Ambiguities', *CineAction!*, 35, 29–40. (Originally published in 1977 in the *Australian Journal of Screen Theory*.)

Perkins, V.F. (1990a) 'Film Authorship: The Premature Burial', *CineAction!*, 21/22, 57–64.

Wood, R. (1988) 'Rancho Notorious: a Noir Western in Colour', *CineAction!*, 13/14, 83–93.

Historical

André Bazin is an important figure in the mise-en-scène tradition who has not explicitly featured in this book. He was a founder editor of *Cahiers du Cinéma*, although he also wrote for numerous other publications including *L'Ecran Français* and *Revue du Cinéma*. The four volumes of criticism collected after his death, *Qu'est-ce que le Cinema?*, were, and have continued to be, very influential. A selection of articles from *Qu'est-ce que le Cinema?* have been translated into English by Hugh Grey and published in two volumes as *What is Cinema?* Several articles are collected in Peter

Graham's *The New Wave*, which also includes criticism of the period by other French writers. Some of the most detailed of Bazin's analysis is found in his writing on Welles and Renoir.

Bazin, A. (1967) *What is Cinema? Volume 1.* Berkeley: University of California Press.
___ (1971) *What is Cinema? Volume 2.* Berkeley: University of California Press.
___ (1973) *Jean Renoir.* New York: Simon & Schuster.
___ (1978) *Orson Welles: A Critical View.* London: Elm Tree Books.
Graham, P. (ed.) (1968) *The New Wave.* London: Secker & Warberg.

Wood, R. (1965) *Hitchcock's Films.* London: Zwemmer.
___ (1989) *Hitchcock's Films Revisited.* New York: Columbia University Press.

A classic of early mise-en-scène criticism and the first book of criticism on Hitchcock written in English. Since 1989 it has been available as part of *Hitchcock's Films Revisited*, a volume which includes the original book together with a collection of Wood's more recent work on the director, much of it excellent. For anyone interested in the way in which Wood's critical approach and, by extension, approaches to film more generally, have changed over the years, the 'Introduction 1988' is very informative. You might also compare the original chapter on *Vertigo* with Chapter 18: 'Male Desire, Male Anxiety: The Essential Hitchcock'.

Barr, C. (1963) 'CinemaScope: Before and After', *Film Quarterly*, 16, 4.

Charles Barr wrote this article after taking advantage of one of the first opportunities to study film in British Higher Education, the annual student-ship offered by the Slade. the articles celebrates the greater opportunities for mise-en-scène that CinemaScope, and the long take, offer film-makers. (A truncated version is reprinted in the third edition (and only the third edition) of G. Mast and M. Cohen (eds) (1985) *Film Theory and Criticism*. Oxford: Oxford University Press.)

Cahiers du Cinéma

Cahiers du Cinéma is still going strong (it recently passed its fiftieth anniversary) although its enthusiasms and approaches have changed more than once since it helped introduce the concept of mise-en-scène. There is a four-volume, translated, collection of articles from *Cahiers* published by Routledge and, more recently, in a paperback edition by Harvard University Press. Of these, the first two volumes, which are on the 1950s and 1960s, edited by Jim Hillier, are the relevant ones. Some of the articles referred to in Chapter 4, here, appear in full, alongside other important work. *Cahiers* criticism is not as detailed or empirical in its approach as *Movie*, but the articles are continually suggestive. Hillier's editorial introductions to the material — one of which is called 'The Apotheosis of *mise en scène*' — are extremely useful.

Hillier, J. (ed.) (1985) *Cahiers du Cinéma: The 1950s*. London: Routledge.
___ (ed.) (1986) *Cahiers du Cinéma: The 1960s*. London: Routledge.

Sequence (and *Sight and Sound*)

As mentioned at the beginning of Chapter 4, the journal *Sequence* contains some eloquent early writing about film authorship and about the quality 'film poetry' which is a similar concept to mise-en-scène. The writing on John Ford provides a privileged example of these critical approaches — as Charles Barr wrote of the *Sequence* critics in 1962 (in an article for Motion, see below), 'Ford was for them a symbol of this poetic quality in the same way that Nicholas Ray is today' (1962b: 40). *Sequence* ran for 14 issues between December 1946 and New Year 1951. Copies can be consulted in the copyright libraries and elsewhere. Articles of particular interest include:

Anderson, L. (1948) 'Creative Elements', *Sequence*, 5, 8–12.
___ (1950a) 'They Were Expendable and John Ford', *Sequence*, 11, 18–31.
___ (1950b) 'The Director's Cinema?', *Sequence*, 12, 6–11, 37.
Ericsson, P. (1947) 'John Ford', *Sequence*, 2, 18–25.

Lambert, G. (1947) 'British Films 1947: Survey and Prospect' *Sequence*, 2, 9–14.
Vaughan, D. (1950) 'On The Town', *Sequence*, 11, 36–8.

For a further discussion of 'poetry', its relationship to mise-en-scène, and the way in which these important debates have been forgotten by the received history of film studies, you could consider my article:

Gibbs, J. (2001) 'Sequence and the archaeology of British film criticism', *Journal of Popular British Cinema*, 4, 14–29.

The debate around authorship expressed in *Sequence* was partly inspired by a number of articles which appeared in *Sight and Sound*, which was edited in the early 1950s by Gavin Lambert (and for which a number of the *Sequence* critics wrote before and after the demise of *Sequence*). The articles in *Sight and Sound*'s authorship debate include:

Dickinson, T. (1950) 'The Filmwright and the Audience', *Sight and Sound*, 19, 1, 20–5.
___ (1950) 'Correspondence: Dickinson v. Koch', *Sight and Sound*, 19:7, 303.
Koch, H. (1950) 'A Playwright Looks at the 'Filmwright'', *Sight and Sound*, 19:5, 210–14.

Oxford Opinion

The relevant issues of *Oxford Opinion* are Nos. 38 (30 April 1960) through 43 (November 1960). *Oxford Opinion* No. 45 (18 February 1961) is a joint issue with *Granta* (No. 1206) which contains an interview with Joseph Losey conducted by Ian Cameron, V.F. Perkins and Mark Shivas.

Definition

The three issues of *Definition* contain two or three really good articles, including the Robin Wood piece 'New Criticism?' quoted in Chapter 4, and also Paddy Whannel's 'Receiving the Message'. Wood's article is not typical of the journal as a whole and has more in common with the ideas espoused in *Oxford Opinion* (of which *Definition* was suspicious, particularly in relation to the films it admired). Edited by Dai Vaughan, Boleslaw Sulik, Alan Lovell and Arnold Wesker, among others, *Definition* aimed to produce 'committed' criticism, but never really gathered momentum partly because of the economic difficulties faced by the small journal, but also because of its failure to grapple with the significance of film style.

Whannel, P. 'Receiving the Message', *Definition*, 3, [Winter 1960/61], 12–15.
Wood, R. 'New Criticism?', *Definition*, 3, [Winter 1960/61], 9–11.

Motion

Like *Movie* and *Definition*, *Motion* is another of the small British film journals of the early 1960s. Its first issue appeared in the summer of 1961 and it published several issues over the next few years albeit (like the others) rather intermittently. *Motion* contains a number of interesting articles including some early work by Charles Barr, a good piece on *The Criminal* by Robin Wood, and an early enthusiastic reception for *Peeping Tom* by Ian Johnson (both No. 5). Raymond Durgnat's witty and irreverent article 'Standing Up For Jesus', from which I quoted briefly in Chapter 4, provides a commentary on the critical battle over the value of film style.

Barr, C. (1962a). 'Nicholas Ray: Adding up the Details', *Motion*, 3, 23–6.
Durgnat, R.(1963) 'Standing up for Jesus', *Motion*, 6, 25–8, 38–42.
Johnson, I. (1963) 'A Pin to see the Peepshow', *Motion*, 4, 36–9.
Wood, R. (1963) 'The Criminal', *Motion*, 4, 7–10.

Monogram

A small journal of a slightly later period (1971–75), which itself grew out of the Brighton Film Review. *Monogram* inherits a concern with mise-en-scène from *Movie*, but combines that with a greater interest in genre and some of the other developments that had overtaken film criticis since 1962. In addition to 'Tales of Sound and Fury', the six issues of *Monogram* include a number of stimulating articles. Issue 4 is devoted to Melodrama.

The melodramatic

In addition to the articles mentioned in chapter 5 (several of which can be found in *Home is Where the Heart is*, the well-known BFI anthology), one might also point to *Movie* 29/30, dedicated to Ophuls and Melodrama, and *Movie* 34/35 which contains a number of important articles including 'Another Look at Sirkian Irony', Deborah Thomas on *Blonde Venus*, Michael Walker on *All I Desire* and Ed Gallafent on *Home from the Hill*.

Babington, B. & P. Evans (1990) 'Another Look at Sirkian Irony', *Movie*, No. 34/35, 47–58.

Elsaesser, T. (1972) 'Tales of Sound and Fury: Observations on the Family Melodrama', *Monogram*, 4, 2–15.

Gledhill, C. (ed.) (1987) *Home is Where the Heart is*. London: BFI.

Halliday, J. (1971) *Sirk on Sirk*. London: BFI/Martin Secker & Warburg. (Second, enlarged edition (1997). London: Faber.)

Mulvey, L. (1977/78) 'Notes on Sirk and Melodrama', *Movie*, 25, 53–6. (Also in Gledhill, ed)

Walker, M. (1982). 'Melodrama and the American Cinema', *Movie*, 29/30, 2–38.

Letter From An Unknown Woman

Letter From An Unknown Woman is not only one of the most accomplished films, it is also one of the best written about. Articles include:

Perkins, V.F. (1982) 'Letter from an Unknown Woman', *Movie*, 29/30, 61–72.

___ (2000a) 'Ophuls Contra Wagner and Others', *Movie*, 36, 73–79.

___ (2000b) 'Same Tune Again!', *CineAction!*, 52, 40–48.

Wilson, G. (1986) *Narration in Light: Studies in Cinematic Point of View*. New York: Johns Hopkins University Press.

Wood, R. (1976) *Personal Views*, London: Gordon Fraser.

___ (1993) 'Letter From an Unknown Woman: The Double Narrative', *CineAction!*, 31, 4–17. Also in R. Wood (1998) *Sexual Politics and Narrative Film: Hollywood and Beyond*. Chichester: Columbia University Press.

Mise-en-scène and point of view

As suggested at the end of Chapter 5, Pye's 'Movies and Point of View' is the perfect place to begin an enquiry into the subject. George M. Wilson's *Narration in Light: Studies in Cinematic Point of View* is one of the most important books of the 1980s. Both Wilson's theoretical discussion, and the analyses of individual films, provide an example of a critic's ability to remind you of the complexity of your experience when cinemagoing. Films which receive major discussion include *Rebel Without a Cause* (Nicholas Ray, 1955), *The Devil is a Woman* (Josef von Sternberg, 1935) and *North by Northwest* (Alfred Hitchcock, 1959). The chapter on *You Only Live Once* (Fritz Lang, 1937) is exceptionally good, but make sure you have seen the film before reading it. Pye's articles on two other Lang films, *The Blue Gardenia* (1953) and *Beyond a Reasonable Doubt* (1956) are also extremely interesting, but again make sure you have seen the films first.

Pye, D. (1988) 'Seeing by Glimpses: Fritz Lang's The Blue Gardenia', *CineAction!*, 13/14, 74–82.
___ (1992) 'Film Noir and Suppressive Narrative: Beyond a Reasonable Doubt' in I. Cameron (ed.) *The Movie Book of Film Noir*. London: Studio Vista, 98–109.
___ (2000) 'Movies and Point of View', *Movie*, 36, 2–34.
Wilson, G. (1986) *Narration in Light: Studies in Cinematic Point of View*. New York: Johns Hopkins University Press.

The philosopher's tradition

Wilson is one of a number of writers with a commitment to film style who come to the subject from a philosophical background. Stanley Cavell, the Walter M. Cabot Professor of Aesthetics and General Theory of Value at Harvard University, is the author of a number of important — and often quite challenging — works including *Pursuits of Happiness* (1981) and *The World Viewed* (1979). The section added to the enlarged edition of *The World Viewed*, 'More of The World Viewed' is a valuable piece of writing on style. William Rothman, author of *Hitchcock: The Murderous Gaze* and *The 'I' of the Camera* is also a philosopher by training. Gilberto Perez, on the other hand, comes to film from theoretical physics — some passages from his wide ranging book *The Material Ghost* were quoted in Chapter 1. Each of the writers share a commitment to detailed analysis and, perhaps because they come from outside the subject area or perhaps because of the nature of their backgrounds, their approach is refreshingly unhampered by the baggage of academic film studies.

Cavell, S. (1979) *The World Viewed: Reflections on the Ontology of Film.* Cambridge MA, London: Harvard University Press.

___ (1981) *Pursuits of Happiness: The Hollywood Comedy of Remarriage.* Cambridge MA, London: Harvard University Press.

___ (1996) *Contesting Tears: The Melodrama of the Unknown Woman.* Chicago: University of Chicago Press.

Perez, G. (1998) *The Material Ghost: Films and their Medium.* Baltimore: Johns Hopkins.

Rothman, W. (1982) *Hitchcock: The Murderous Gaze.* Harvard University Press.

___ (1988) *The 'I' of the Camera: Essays in Film Criticism, History, and Aesthetics.* Cambridge: Cambridge University Press.

___ (1997) *Documentary Film Classics.* Cambridge: Cambridge University Press.

BFI Classics

The BFI Classics series, and also the 'Modern Classics', has provided the opportunity for sustained analysis of individual films. Surprisingly few of the authors have taken up this invitation, however, many deciding to discuss aspects of the film's production or reception. There are nevertheless some excellent titles in the range, including: V.F. Perkins on *The Magnificent Ambersons*, Camille Paglia on *The Birds*, and Laura Mulvey on *Citizen Kane*.

Some Recent Books

In distinction to the excessive expressive mode of melodrama, Andrew Klevan's *Disclosure of the Everyday* is concerned with films and directors which work in smaller registers. The book considers the way in which directors such as Yasujiro Ozu, Robert Bresson and Eric Rohmer have worked creatively by operating within self-imposed constraints and by addressing the significance of everyday experience.

Deborah Thomas, mentioned earlier in connection with *Movie* has recently published two books. The first is *Beyond Genre* (Cameron & Hollis), which was referred to in Chapter 5. In the course of an investigation of the interplay of the 'comedic', the 'melodramatic' and the 'romantic', Thomas analyses a number of films, including *Schindler's List*, *Monkey Business*, *The Palm Beach Story* and *An Affair to Remember*. The second is *Reading Hollywood: Spaces and Meanings in American Film*, another title in the Short Cuts series, which brings a detailed style-based approach — with particular emphasis on space, setting and décor — to bear on *My Darling Clementine*, *Party Girl*, *Advise and Consent* and others.

Susan Smith's new work on Hitchcock not only includes a chapter entitled 'Mise-en-scène', but also, as its title suggests, focuses on 'tone' in its discussion of the director's work. Tone is an important and neglected concept in thinking about film. The term's roots lie in 'tone of voice', the way that how something is said indicates to the listener how it is to be understood. The literary critic Wayne C. Booth, in *The Rhetoric of Fiction*, defines tone as 'the implicit evaluation which the author manages to convey behind his explicit presentation' (1961: 74). Douglas Pye argues that tone 'is one of the central ways in which a film can signal how we are to take what we see and hear; it points to both our relationship to the film and the film's relationship to its material and its conventions.' (2000: 17).

Klevan, A. (2000) *Disclosure of the Everyday: Undramatic Achievement in Narrative Film*. Trowbridge: Flicks Books.

Smith, S. (2000) *Hitchcock: Suspense, Humour and Tone*. London: BFI.

Thomas, D. (2000) *Beyond Genre*. Moffat: Cameron & Hollis.

___ (2001) *Reading Hollywood: Spaces and Meanings in American Film*. London: Wallflower Press.

NOTES

CHAPTER 1

[1] I had the good fortune to study this sequence in one of the ever-stimulating classes of Douglas Pye, at the University of Reading. When, more recently, I discussed these critical perspectives with him, he wanted to acknowledge the importance of teaching the film with Laura Mulvey and the quality of her insight on the film. Tania Modleski also discusses the shot in her chapter on *Notorious* in *The Women Who Knew Too Much* (1988: 60, 66–7) in which she challenges Michael Renov's earlier comments (1980: 32).

[2] The word figure is here being used in a similar way to 'figure of speech' or 'figure of eight'. A point of view figure refers to the three shots necessary to unambiguously establish that we are, in the middle of the three, enjoying the same perspective as the character concerned. In other words, this grouping of shots includes a middle shot in which the camera takes up the same position as the character's head, and two shots of the character looking (usually out of the frame) which bookend the central shot.

[3] Perez's account is misleading in one particular: the shot which he describes as being 'from his point of view' is static whilst Johnnie/Keaton

is moving rapidly through space on the tender. The composition of the shot reflects the angle at which he is looking, and it certainly shows the space behind the camera, but it is not a point of view shot.

CHAPTER 2

[1]   The other kind of border film which might be worth mentioning here are three films of Jean Renoir — *Le Crime de Monsieur Lange* (1935), *La Grande Illusion* (1937) and *La Règle du Jeu* (1939).

[2]   It may also be worth remembering the earlier scene where Danny (Jesse Borrego), the journalist, claims that it was only in order to profit from slavery that Texas fought for its independence from Mexico, although Pilar Cruz (Elizabeth Peña) suggests that this is a somewhat partial view.

[3]   As we will consider in Chapter 3, the significance a critic can attribute to any technique is dependent on its context and what it is helping to express. In the same article, Wood explores the way *Touch of Evil* also 'uses editing repeatedly to underline the sense of connectedness established by the camera style' (1976: 143).

[4]   Or to quote Sayles, writer, editor and director of *Lone Star*, 'A cut is very much a tear. You use a cut to say there's a separation between this thing and that thing. And so in *Lone Star* I didn't even want a dissolve, which is a soft cut' (quoted in Smith 1998: 230).

[5]   The fact that Sam chooses to travel across the border to meet Chucho, rather than to telephone, as Ray his less sympathetic deputy suggests, shows a recognition on Sam's part that the only possible way to discover this history, hidden by the official records, is to approach Chucho on a personal level.

[6]   Some of these choices fall within the field of editing, and perhaps therefore outside the terms of this enquiry. See Chapter 4 for a discussion

of the relationship between mise-en-scène and editing.

CHAPTER 3

¹ Gombrich (1966: 71) and Wimsatt (Wimsatt and Beardsley 1954: 81) cite Aristotle as the root of these ideas. The *Oxford Companion to Art* also mentions the *Poetics*, but under the entry 'Organic', suggests that Plato's *Phaedrus* provides an earlier example (Osborne 1970: 795).

² Sometimes you will come across the phrase 'recurring motif', but this (at least in some senses of 'motif') is tautological. 'Motif' tends to be defined differently in the context of different art forms, and may not — in the case of music, for example — involve the visual at all.

³ Noel Carroll makes a similar distinction in referring to 'horizontal coherence' and 'vertical coherence' in his discussion of V.F. Perkins' *Film as Film* in *Philosophical Problems of Classical Film Theory*: 'In discussing the unity of a film, we can draw a distinction between at least two species of film coherence. We might speak of its coherence over time, the intelligibility of its linear organization. This would be analogous to the developmental structure of a piece of music or a musical form, for example the sonata allegro. We might dub this, "horizontal coherence". On the other hand a film might be said to be coherent in virtue of the unity or harmony or integration within one or more of its parts. ... Let us call this "vertical coherence".' (1988: 237–8)

⁴ Lindsay Anderson, for example, employed this name in a review of *Birth of a Nation* (1953: 129–30).

⁵ Interview, 19 June 1997. Included in J. Gibbs 1999: 230.

⁶ In fairness to Lindgren, he also stresses the importance of recognising the relationship between one shot and those that surround it, but this

is partly a reflection of the commitment of 'Film Appreciation' to the centrality of editing over other areas of film-making.

[7] Perhaps in this the authors are trying to respect the term's theatrical origins, or perhaps their approach is a vestige of the once influential distinction in film theory between the 'profilmic event' and the 'filmic codes'?

CHAPTER 4

[1] For the record, Wood's piece is not typical of the articles which appeared in *Definition*. An editorial explains that the writers have decided to publish 'New Criticism?' because it contains 'in its positive passages a summary of all that is really valuable in the "right wing" attitude as represented in this country mainly by *Oxford Opinion*'. (1960/61: 3)

[2] Equally, regarding my earlier comments on *Sequence* and that journal's use of the term 'poetry', Wood's description of the role of the director is very similar to the views expressed by Lindsay Anderson in 1948: 'Good films, the purest and the best, speak through camera work — composition and flow of images — as much as through the words spoken by the characters or the "literary" significance of the plot. Style and content fuse to form something new, something individual, a whole greater than its parts. A synopsis of *L'Atalante* means as little as one of a lyric poem; on paper *My Darling Clementine* is just another Western. But as they unfold upon the screen, with grace of movement, freshness of vision, they are found to possess a magic power to excite, to enchant, to revive. To describe this as "formal beauty" is inadequate and misleading, for the phrase implies the frigid sterile formality of a work like *Day of Wrath*, rather than the living poetry which is the result when even a commonplace story is given shape and meaning by an expressive camera, sympathetic music and design, skilled actors, and above all by creative direction — direction which gathers all these elements together, and gives them unity and life.

So in this gathering together, this fusion, there must be a central figure, one man conscious of the relative significance of every shot, the shape and flow of every sequence. But he cannot stand alone; he stands with, dependent on, his author and his cameraman. No doubt in an ideal world the same man would fulfil each function, but it is no use writing criticism for an ideal world.' (1948: 9)

3   See 'A Guide to Current Films', *Sight and Sound*, 24, 4, 214.

4   I. Cameron (1960d) 'Los Angeles Mon Amour', *Oxford Opinion*, 40, 35–6; M. Shivas (1960b) *'Home from the Hill'*, *Oxford Opinion*, 43, 34–5; I. Cameron (1960a) *'Comanche Station'*, *Oxford Opinion*, 38, 41; V.F. Perkins (1960b) 'Charm and Blood', *Oxford Opinion*, 42, 34–5; I. Cameron (1960c) 'Frank Tashlin', *Oxford Opinion*, 39, 33–6.

5   Interview, 19 June 1997. Included in J. Gibbs 1999: 222–3.

6   Or, as the editors of *Oxford Opinion* wrote to *The Spectator*, which had uncritically picked up some of Houston's remarks: 'Style is not just an embellishment; it is the method by which meaning is expressed. Miss Houston writes that the cinema is "not about spatial relationships". We never said it was. But human relationships can be expressed in spatial terms.' I. Cameron, V.F. Perkins & M. Shivas 'Commitment in Films', *The Spectator*, 14 Oct 1960, 561.

7   This comment appears in the round table discussion by members of the *Cahiers* editorial board: 'Hiroshima, notre amour', *Cahiers du Cinéma*, 97, (July 1959), translated in Hillier, 1985: 59–70. As Hillier points out in a footnote, Luc Moullet 'had already pronounced that "morality is a question of tracking shots"' (Hillier 1985: 69) in his article 'Sam Fuller: sur les brisées de Marlowe', *Cahiers du Cinéma*, 93, (March 1959), also translated in Hillier (1985: 145–55).

CHAPTER 5

¹ An almost identical set of circumstances applied in England, with the restrictions ending not with the revolution as was the case in France, but with the Theatre Regulation Act of 1843.

² Eliot observes that: 'In *The Moonstone* Collins succeeds in bringing into play those aids of 'atmosphere' in which Dickens (and the Brontës) exhibited such genius, and in which Collins has everything except their genius. For his purpose, he does not come off badly. Compare the description of the discovery of Rosanna's death in the Shivering Sands — and notice how carefully, beforehand, the *mise-en-scène* of the Shivering Sands is prepared for us — with the shipwreck of Steerforth in David Copperfield' (1932: 465). Eliot might appear to be using the term in the transferred, figurative sense mentioned by the OED — 'The setting, surroundings, or background of an event or action'. But Eliot is not merely talking about background, nor employing the term neutrally. That the Shivering Sands have been 'prepared for us' suggests something of the idea of staging. In the context of the essay, which is intimately concerned with drama (or rather melodrama in which Dickens and Collins were, as Eliot takes pains to make clear, actively involved) then the theatrical origins of the term are inevitably invoked. Most importantly, however, the mise-en-scène of the Shivering Sands is one of the 'aids of atmosphere' which Eliot is celebrating. It is not merely the background, but a means of expression itself — and the object of Eliot's admiration.

³ *The Courtship of Eddie's Father* receives an extended analysis in Thomas' *Beyond Genre* (2000), which includes much discussion of the interplay of melodramatic and comedic elements.

⁴ I have taken this quote from the revised version of 'Tales of Sound and Fury' which appears in anthologies (such as Gledhill's). The original, from the parentheses, reads: 'and a 'thematisation' of objects which develop the existentialist antithesis of the individual in a closed society into the

more directly philosophical point about a world totally predetermined and pervaded by 'meaning' and interpretable signs.' (1972: 13)

5   For a fuller discussion of the two Willemen articles, and Laura Mulvey's 'Notes on Sirk and Melodrama', see Gibbs 1999.

CHAPTER 6

1   Similar disjunctions happen outside the home as well. When Sarah Jane or Annie leave the house they move in an urban, night-time world but when Susie ventures outside she is surrounded by rolling hills and greenery.

2   'Universal didn't interfere with either my camera work or my cutting — which meant a lot to me' (Halliday 1997: 97).

CONCLUSION

1   See J. Gibbs 1999, 2001. Colin McArthur makes a similar suggestion in his BFI Classic on *The Big Heat* (1992: 11, 49).

BIBLIOGRAPHY

Anderson, L. (1948) 'Creative Elements' *Sequence*, 5, 8–12.

____ (1950a) *'They Were Expendable* and John Ford', *Sequence*, 11, 18–31.

____ (1950b) 'The Director's Cinema?', *Sequence*, 12, 6–11, 37.

____ (1953) *'Birth of a Nation'*, *Sight and Sound*, 22, 3, 129–30.

Astruc, A. (1948) 'The Birth of a new avant-garde: La caméra-stylo', *Ecran Français*, 144, translated in P. Graham (ed.) (1968) *The New Wave*. London: Secker & Warberg.

Babington, B. and P. Evans (1990) 'Another Look at Sirkian Irony', *Movie*, 34/35 (Winter), 47–58.

Barr, C. (1962a) 'Nicholas Ray: adding up the details', *Motion*, 3, 23–6.

____ (1962b) 'Le Film Maudit', *Motion*, 3, 38–40.

____ (1963) 'CinemaScope: Before and After', *Film Quarterly*, 16, 4.

____ (1999) *English Hitchcock*. Moffat: Cameron & Hollis.

Bazin, A. (1967) *What is Cinema? Volume 1*. Berkeley: University of California Press.

____ (1971) *What is Cinema? Volume 2*. Berkeley: University of California Press.

____ (1973) *Jean Renoir*. New York: Simon & Schuster.

____ (1978) *Orson Welles: A Critical View*. London: Elm Tree Books.

Booth, W. (1961) *The Rhetoric of Fiction*. London: University of Chicago Press.

Boys, B. (1963) *'The Courtship of Eddie's Father'*, *Movie*, 10, 29–32.

Britton, A. (1976) *'Mandingo'*, *Movie*, 22, 1–22.

____ (1983). *Cary Grant: Comedy and Male Desire*. Newcastle: Tyneside Cinema.

____ (1991/92). 'A New Servitude: Bette Davis, *Now Voyager* and the Radicalism of the Woman's Film', *CineAction!*, 26/27, 32–59.

____ (1993) *'Meet Me in St Louis*: Smith, or the Ambiguities', *CineAction!*, 35, 29–40.

____ (1995) *Katharine Hepburn: Star as Feminist*. London: Studio Vista.

Brooks, P. (1976) *The Melodramatic Imagination: Balzac, Henry James, Melodrama, and the Mode of Excess*. London: Yale University Press.

Byatt, A.S. (2000) *On Histories and Stories: Selected Essays*. London: Chatto & Windus.

Cameron, I. (1960a) 'Films', *Oxford Opinion*, 38, 36.

____ (1960b) *'Comanche Station'*, *Oxford Opinion*, 38, 41.

_____ (1960c) 'Frank Tashlin', *Oxford Opinion*, 39, 33–6.

_____ (1960d) 'Los Angeles Mon Amour', *Oxford Opinion*, 40, 35–6.

_____ (1960e) 'Flores Parlos Muertos', *Oxford Opinion*, 41, 42–6.

_____ (1962a) 'Films, Directors and Critics', *Movie*, 2, 4–7.

_____ (1962b) 'Hitchcock 1: and the Mechanics of Suspense', *Movie*, 3, 4–7.

_____ (1963) 'Hitchcock 2: Suspense and Meaning', *Movie*, 6, 8–12.

_____ (ed.) (1972) *Movie Reader*. London: November Books.

_____ (ed.) (1992) *The Movie Book of Film Noir*. London: Studio Vista.

Cameron, I., V.F. Perkins & M. Shivas (1960) 'Commitment in Films', *The Spectator*, 14 October, 561.

Cameron, I. & D. Pye (eds) (1996) *The Movie Book of the Western*. London: Studio Vista.

Carroll, N. (1988) *Philosophical Problems of Classical Film Theory*. Oxford: Princetown University Press.

Cavell, S. (1979) *The World Viewed: Reflections on the Ontology of Film*. Cambridge MA, London: Harvard University Press.

_____ (1981) *Pursuits of Happiness: The Hollywood Comedy of Remarriage*. Cambridge MA, London: Harvard University Press.

_____ (1996) *Contesting Tears: The Melodrama of the Unknown Woman*. Chicago: University of Chicago Press.

Dickinson, T. (1950) 'The Filmwright and the Audience', *Sight and Sound*, 19, 1, 20–5.

_____ (1950) 'Correspondence: Dickinson v. Koch', *Sight and Sound*, 19, 7, 303.

Durgnat, R. (1963) 'Standing up for Jesus', *Motion*, 6, 25–8, 38–42.

Dyer, R. (1981) 'Minnelli's Web of Dreams', *The Movie*, Ch. 58, (Reprinted in A. Lloyd (ed.) *Movies of the Fifties*. London: Orbis Publishing, 1982, 86–89).

_____ (1977/78) 'Four Films of Lana Turner', *Movie*, 25, 30–52.

Editors of *Cahiers* (1959) 'Hiroshima, notre amour', *Cahiers du Cinéma*, 97, translated in J. Hillier (ed.) *Cahiers du Cinéma: The 1950s*, 1985, 59–70.

Editors of *Definition* [1960 / 61] 'Editorial', *Definition*, 3, 3–6.

Editors of *Sight and Sound* (1958) 'A Guide to Current Films', *Sight and Sound*, 24, 4, 214.

Eliot, T.S. (1932) *Selected Essays*. London: Faber & Faber.

Elsaesser, T. (1972) 'Tales of Sound and Fury: Observations on the Family Melodrama', *Monogram*, 4, 2–15.

Ericsson, P. (1947) 'John Ford', *Sequence*, 2, 18–25.

Fassbinder, R. W. (1972) 'Six films by Douglas Sirk' in J. Halliday & L. Mulvey (eds) *Douglas Sirk*. Edinburgh: Edinburgh Film Festival.

Gallafent, E. (1990) 'The Adventures of Rafe Hunnicut: The Bourgeois Family in *Home from the Hill*', *Movie*, 34/35, 65–81.

_____ (2000) *Astaire & Rogers*. Moffat: Cameron & Hollis.

Gibbs, J. (1999) *'It Was Never All in the Script...': Mise-en-scène and the Interpretation of Visual Style in British Film Journals, 1946–78*, unpublished PhD thesis, University of Reading.

_____ (2001) *'Sequence* and the archaeology of British film criticism', *Journal of Popular British Cinema*, 4, 14–29.

Gledhill, C. (ed.) (1987) *Home is Where the Heart is*. London: BFI.

Gombrich, E.H. (1966) *Norm and Form*. London: Phaidon.

Graham, P. (ed.) (1968) *The New Wave*. London: Secker & Warberg.

Halliday, J. (1997) *Sirk on Sirk* (2nd edn.). London: BFI/Martin Secker & Warburg.

Hemming, J. (1983) *The Conquest of the Incas*. Harmondsworth: Penguin.

Hillier, J. (ed.) (1985) *Cahiers du Cinéma: The 1950s*. London: Routledge.

____ (ed.) (1986) *Cahiers du Cinéma: The 1960s*. London: Routledge.

Houston, P. (1960) 'The Critical Question', *Sight and Sound*, 29, 4, 160–5.

Hoveyda, F. (1960a) 'Nicholas Ray's Reply: *Party Girl*', *Cahiers du Cinéma*, 107, translated in J. Hillier (ed.) (1986) Cahiers du Cinéma: The 1960's, 122–131.

____ (1960b) 'Les Taches du Soleil', *Cahiers du Cinéma*, 110, translated as 'Sunspots' in J. Hillier (ed.) (1986) *Cahiers du Cinéma: The 1960s*, 135–45.

Jacobowitz, F. (1986) 'Feminist Film Theory and Social Reality', *CineAction!*, 3/4, 21–31.

Johnson, I. (1963) 'A Pin to see the Peepshow', *Motion*, 4, 36–9.

Klevan, A. (2000). *Disclosure of the Everyday: Undramatic Achievement in Narrative Film*. Trowbridge: Flicks Books.

Koch, H. (1950) 'A Playwright Looks at the "Filmwright"', *Sight and Sound*, 19, 5, 210–14.

Lambert, G. (1947) 'British Films 1947: Survey and Prospect' *Sequence*, 2, 9–14.

____ (1952) 'A Last Look Round', *Sequence*, 14, 4–8.

Lindgren, E. (1948) *The Art of the Film*. London: George Allen & Unwin.

Lloyd, A, (ed.) (1982) *Movies of the Fifties*. London: Orbis Publishing.

Lehman, P. and W. Luhr (1977) *Authorship and Narrative in the Cinema*. New York: Putnam.

Mayersberg, P. (1963) '*The Trial of Joan of Arc*', *Movie*, 7, 30–2.

McArthur, C. (1992) *The Big Heat*. London: BFI.

Modleski, T. (1988) *The Women Who Knew Too Much: Hitchcock and Feminist Film Theory*. New York, London: Methuen.

Moullet, L. (1959) 'Sam Fuller: sur les brisées de Marlowe', *Cahiers du Cinéma*, 93, translated in J. Hillier (ed.) (1985) Cahiers du Cinéma: The 1950's, 145–55.

Mulvey, L. (1977/78) 'Notes on Sirk and Melodrama', *Movie*, 25, 53–6.

____ (1992) *Citizen Kane*. London: BFI.

____ (1996) *Fetishism and Curiosity*. London: BFI.

Osborne, H. (ed.) (1970) *Oxford Companion to Art*. Oxford: Oxford University Press.

Paglia, C. (1998) *The Birds*. London: BFI.

Perez, G. (1998) *The Material Ghost: Films and their Medium*. Baltimore: Johns Hopkins University Press.

Perkins, V.F. (1960a) 'Nicholas Ray', *Oxford Opinion*, 40, 31–34.

____ (1960b) 'Charm and Blood', *Oxford Opinion*, 42, 34–5.

____ (1962a) (on behalf of the editorial board) 'The British Cinema', *Movie*, 1, 2–7.

____ (1962b) '*River of no Return*', *Movie*, 2, 18–9.

____ (1963a) '*Rope*', *Movie*, 7, 11–13.

____ (1963b) 'The Cinema of Nicholas Ray', Movie, 9, 4–10.

____ (1972) *Film as Film: Understanding and Judging Movies*. Harmondsworth: Penguin.

____ (1981) 'Moments of Choice', *The Movie*, Ch. 58, 1141–5 (Reprinted in A. Lloyd (ed.) (1982) *Movies of the Fifties*. London: Orbis Publishing, 209–13).

____ (1982) '*Letter from an Unknown Woman*', *Movie*, 29/30, 61–72.

____ (1990a) 'Film Authorship: The Premature Burial', *CineAction!*, 21/22, 57–64.

____ (1990b) 'Must We Say What They Mean?: Film Criticism and Interpretation', *Movie*, 34/35, 1–6.

____ (1999) *The Magnificent Ambersons*. London: BFI.

____ (2000a) 'Ophuls Contra Wagner and Others', *Movie*, 36, 73–9.

____ (2000b) 'Same Tune Again!', *CineAction!*, 52, 40–8.

Place, J. and J. Burton (1976) 'Feminist Film Criticism', *Movie*, 22, 53–62.

Pye, D. (1975) '*Junior Bonner*', *Movie*, 21, 22–5.

____ (1988) 'Seeing by Glimpses: Fritz Lang's *The Blue Gardenia*', *CineAction!*, 13/14, 74–82.

____ (1989) 'Bordwell and Hollywood', *Movie*, 33, 46–52.

____ (1992) 'Film Noir and Suppressive Narrative: *Beyond a Reasonable Doubt*' in I. Cameron (ed.) *The Movie Book of Film Noir*. London: Studio Vista, 98–109.

____ (2000) 'Movies and Point of View', *Movie*, 36, 2–34.

Ray, N. (1956) 'Story into Script', *Sight and Sound*, 26, 2, 70–4.

Renov, M. (1980) 'From Identification to Ideology: The Male System of Hitchcock's *Notorious*', *Wide Angle*, 4, 30–7.

Rothman, W. (1982) *Hitchcock: The Murderous Gaze*. Harvard University Press.

____ (1988) *The 'I' of the Camera: Essays in Film Criticism, History, and Aesthetics*. Cambridge: Cambridge University Press.

____ (1997) *Documentary Film Classics*. Cambridge: Cambridge University Press.

Sayles, J. (1998). *Men with Guns & Lone Star*. London: Faber & Faber.

Shivas, M. (1960a) 'The Commercial Cinema: a few basic principles', *Oxford Opinion*, 38, 38–40.

____ (1960b) '*Home from the Hill*', *Oxford Opinion*, 43, 34–5.

____ (1963) 'In Paris: *Landru, The Trial*'. *Movie*, 7, 7–10.

Smith, G. (ed.) (1998) *Sayles on Sayles*. London: Faber & Faber.

Smith, S. (2000) *Hitchcock: Suspense, Humour and Tone*. London: BFI.

Thomas, D. (1990). '*Blonde Venus*', *Movie*, 34/35, 7–15.

____ (2000) *Beyond Genre*. Moffat: Cameron & Hollis.

____ (2001) *Reading Hollywood: Spaces and Meanings in American Film*. London: Wallflower Press.

Vaughan, D. (1950) '*On The Town*', *Sequence*, 11, 36–8.

Walker, M. (1982). 'Melodrama and the American Cinema', *Movie*, 29/30, 2–38.

____ (1990) '*All I Desire*', *Movie*, 34/35, 31–47.

Whannel, P. (1960/61) 'Receiving the Message', *Definition*, 3, 12–15.

Willett, J. (1964, 1978) *Brecht on Theatre*. London: Methuen.

Wilson, G. (1986) *Narration in Light: Studies in Cinematic Point of View*. New York: Johns Hopkins University Press.

Willemen, P. (1971) 'Distanciation and Douglas Sirk', *Screen*, 12: 2, 63–7.

____ (1972/73) 'Towards an Analysis of the Sirkian system', *Screen*, 13:4, 128–34.

Willett, J. (ed.) (1964, 1978) *Brecht on Theatre*. London: Methuen.

Wimsatt, W. K. and M. Beardsley (1954) *The Verbal Icon*. Kentucky: University of Kentucky Press.

Wood, R. (1960/61) 'New Criticism?', *Definition*, 3, 9–11.

____ (1963) '*The Criminal*', *Motion*, 4, 7–10.

____ (1965) *Hitchcock's Films*. London: Zwemmer.

____ (1975) 'Smart-ass & Cutie-pie: Notes toward and evaluation of Altman', *Movie*, 21, 1–17.

____ (1976) *Personal Views*. London: Gordon Fraser.

____ (1986) 'Editorial', *CineAction!*, 3/4, 1–2.

____ (1988). 'Rancho Notorious: a Noir Western in Colour', *CineAction!*, 13/14, 83–93.

____ (1989) *Hitchcock's Films Revisited*. New York: Columbia University Press.

____ (1993) '*Letter From an Unknown Woman*: The Double Narrative', *CineAction!*, 31, 4–17.

____ (1998) *Sexual Politics and Narrative Film: Hollywood and Beyond*. Chichester: Columbia University Press.

INDEX

THE SHORT CUTS SERIES

The SHORT CUTS series is a comprehensive library of introductory texts covering the full spectrum of Film Studies, including genres, critical concepts, film histories/movements, and film technologies.

With concise discussion of contemporary issues within historical and cultural context and the extensive use of illustrative case studies, this list of study guides is perfectly suited to building an individually-styled library for all students and enthusiasts of cinema and popular culture.

The series will grow to over forty titles; listed here are the first waves of this ambitious attempt to systematically treat all the major areas of undergraduate Film Studies.

"This series is tailor-made for a modular approach to film studies ... an indispensable tool for both lecturers and students."

Paul Willemen, University of Ulster

01   THE HORROR GENRE
FROM BEELZEBUB TO BLAIR WITCH

Paul Wells   ISBN 1-903364-00-0   144pp

The inaugral book in the *Short Cuts* series is a comprehensive introduction to the history and key themes of the horror genre. The main issues and debates raised by horror, and the approaches and theories that have been applied to horror texts are all addressed. In charting the evolution of the horror film in social and cultural context, Paul Wells explores how it has reflected and commented upon particular historical periods, and asks how it may respond to the new millennium by citing recent innovations in the genre's development, such as the 'urban myth' narrative underpinning *Candyman* and *The Blair Witch Project*.

"An informed and highly readable account that is theoretically broad, benefiting from a wide range of cinematic examples."

Xavier Mendik, University College Northampton

02 THE STAR SYSTEM
HOLLYWOOD'S PRODUCTION OF POPULAR IDENTITIES

Paul McDonald
ISBN 1-903364-02-7   144pp

The Star System looks at the development and changing organization of the star system in the American film industry. Tracing the popularity of star performers from the early 'cinema of attractions' to the internet universe, Paul McDonald explores the ways in which Hollywood has made and sold its stars. Through focusing on particular historical periods, the key conditions influencing the star system in silent cinema, the studioera and the New Hollywood are discussed and illustrated by cases studies of Mary Pickford, Bette Davis, James Cagney, Julia Roberts, Tom Cruise, and Will Smith.

"A very good introduction to the topic filling an existing gap in the needs of researchers and students of the subject."

Roberta Pearson, University of Wales, Cardiff

03 SCIENCE FICTION CINEMA
FROM OUTERSPACE TO CYBERSPACE

Geoff King and Tanya Krzywinska
ISBN 1-903364-03-5   144pp

Science Fiction Cinema charts the dimensions of one of the most popular film genres. From lurid comic-book blockbusters to dark dystopian visions, science fiction is seen as both a powerful cultural barometer of our times and the product of particular industrial and commercial frameworks. The authors outline the major themes of the genre, from representations of the mad scientist and computer hacker to the relationship between science fiction and postmodernism, exploring issues such as the meaning of special effects and the influence of science fiction cinema on the entertainment media of the digital age.

"The best overview of English-language science-fiction cinema published to date... thorough, clearly written and full of excellent examples. Highly recommended."

Steve Neale, Sheffield Hallam University

04 EARLY SOVIET CINEMA
INNOVATION. IDEOLOGY AND PROPAGANDA.

David Gillespie
ISBN 1-903364-04-3   144pp

Early Soviet Cinema examines the aesthetics of Soviet cinema during its 'golden age' of the 1920s, against a background of cultural ferment and the construction of a new socialist society. Separate chapters are devoted to the work of Sergei Eisenstein, Lev Kuleshov, Vsevolod Pudovkin, Dziga Vertov and Alexander Dovzhenko. Other major directors are also discussed at length. David Gillespie places primary focus on the text, with analysis concentrating on the artistic qualities, rather than the political implications, of each film. The result is not only a discussion of each director's contribution to the 'golden age' and to world cinema, but also an exploration of their own distinctive poetics.

"An excellent book ... Lively and informative, it fills a significant gap and deserves to be on reading lists wherever courses on Soviet cinema are run."

Graham Roberts, University of Surrey

05   READING HOLLYWOOD
SPACES AND MEANINGS IN AMERICAN FILM

Deborah Thomas   ISBN 1-903364-01-9   144pp

Reading Hollywood examines the treatment of space and narrative in a selection of classic films including *My Darling Clementine*, *Its a Wonderful Life* and *Vertigo*. Deborah Thomas employs a variety of arguments in exploring the reading of space and its meaning in Hollywood cinema, and film generally. Topics covered include the importance of space in defining genre (such as the necessity of an urban landscape for a gangster film to be a gangster film); the ambiguity of offscreen space and spectatorship (how an audience reads an unseen but inferred setting) and the use of spatially disruptive cinematic techniques such as flashback to construct meaning.

"Amongst the finest introductions to Hollywood in particular and Film Studies in general ... subtler, more complex, yet more readable than most of its rivals, many of which it will displace."

Professor Robin Wood, *CineAction!*

06   DISASTER MOVIES
THE CINEMA OF CATASTROPHE

Stephen Keane   ISBN 1-903364-05-1   144pp

Disaster Movies provides a comprehensive introduction to the history and development of the disaster genre. The 1950s sci-fi B-movies to high concept 1990s 'millennial movies', Stephen Keane looks at the ways in which the representation of disaster and its aftermath are borne out of both contextual considerations and the increasing commercial demands of contemporary Hollywood. Through detailed analyses of such films as *Airport*, *The Poseidon Adventure*, *Independence Day* and *Titanic*, the book explores the continual reworking of this, to-date, undervalued genre.

"Providing detailed consideration of key movies within their social and cultural context, this concise introduction serves its purpose well and should prove a useful teaching tool."

Nick Roddick

07   THE WESTERN GENRE
FROM LORDSBURG TO BIG WHISKEY

John Saunders   ISBN 1-903364-12-4   144pp

The Western Genre offers close readings of the definitive American film movement as represented by such leading exponents as John Ford, Howard Hawks and Sam Peckinpah. In his consideration of such iconic motifs as the Outlaw Hero and the *Lone Rider*, John Saunders traces the development of perennial aspects of the genre, its continuity and, importantly, its change. Representations of morality and masculinity are also foregrounded in consideration of the genres major stars John Wayne and Clint Eastwood, and the book includes a number of detailed analyses of such landmark films as *Shane, Rio Bravo*, *The Wild Bunch* and *Unforgiven*.

"A clear exposition of the major thematic currents of the genre providing attentive and illuminating reading of major examples."

Ed Buscombe, Editor of the BFI Companion to the Werstern

08 PSYCHOANALYSIS AND CINEMA
THE PLAY OF SHADOWS

Vicky Lebeau

ISNB 1-903364-19-1   144pp

The book examines the long and uneven history of developments in modern art, science and technology that brought pychoanalysis and the cinema together towards the end of the nineteenth century. Vicky Lebeau explores the subsequent encounters between the two: the seductions of psychoanalysis and cinema as converging, though distinct, ways of talking about dream and desire, image and illusion, shock and sexuality. Beginning with Freud's encounter with the spectacle of hysteria on display in fin-de-siècle Paris, this study offers a detailed reading of the texts and concepts which generated the field of psychoanalytic film theory.

"A very lucid and subtle exploration of the reception of Freud's theories and their relation to psychoanalysis's contemporary developments - cinema and modernism. One of the best introduction to psychoanalytic film' theory available."

Elizabeth Cowie, University of Kent

09 COSTUME AND CINEMA
DRESS CODES IN POPULAR FILM

Sarah Street

1-903364-18-3   144pp

Costume and Cinema presents an overview of the literature on film costume, together with a series of detailed case studies which highlight how costume is a key signifier in film texts. Sarah Street demonstrates how costume relates in fundamental ways to the study of film narrative and mise-en-scène, in some cases constituting a language of its own. In particular the book foregrounds the related issues of adaptation and embodiment in a variety of different genres and films including *Desperately Seeking Susan, Titanic* and *The Matrix*.

"A valuable addition to the growing literature on film and costume ... engagingly written, offering a lucid introduction to the field."

Stella Bruzzi, Royal Holloway, University of London

11 NEW CHINESE CINEMA
CHALLENGING REPRESENTATIONS

Sheila Cornelius with Ian Haydn Smith

1-903364-13-2   144pp

New Chinese Cinema examines the 'search for roots' films that emerged from China in the aftermath of the Cultural Revolution. The authors contextualise the films of the so-called Fifth Generation directors who came to prominence in the 1980s and 1990s such as Chen Kaige, Zhang Yimou and Tian Zhuangzhuang. Including close analysis of such pivotal films as *Farewell My Concubine*, *Raise the Red Lantern* and *The Blue Kite*, the book also examines the rise of contemporary Sixth Generation underground directors whose themes embrace the disaffection of urban youth.

"Very thorough in its coverage of the historical and cultural background to New Chinese Cinema ... clearly written and appropriately targeted at an undergraduate audience."

Leon Hunt, Brunel University